Chambers
spell it yourself!

G T Hawker

Chambers

CHAMBERS

An imprint of Chambers Harrap Publishers Ltd

7 Hopetoun Crescent

Edinburgh, EH7 4AY

First published by Chambers Harrap Publishers Ltd 2007

ISBN 978 0550 10346 8

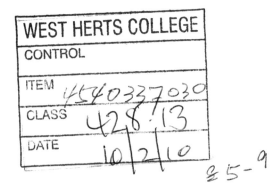
Designed and typeset by Chambers Harrap Publishers Ltd, Edinburgh

Printed in Slovenia by arrangement with
Associated Agencies Ltd Oxford

Contents

Contributors

Compiler

Gordon T Hawker

Editor

Mary O'Neill

Editorial Assistance

Vicky Aldus

Data Management

Gerry Breslin

Prepress

Heather Macpherson

Note for teachers and parents

Spell It Yourself is based on the belief that there is a need for a different type of book to help children with their spelling, one which is neither a dictionary nor a conventional spelling book.

Most children are encouraged to refer to dictionaries for spellings of words they wish to use in their written work. But a school dictionary will contain many words and definitions which children already know and can spell, for example *cat, dog, pig, and,* etc. And school dictionaries have been compiled, in the first place, for the giving of definitions. A child might wish to spell and write such words as *banana, biscuit* or *chocolate,* but would not need their definitions; he or she would already know the words. In their written compositions, children use words whose meanings they understand, therefore they do not often need the definitions of the words they want to spell.

Also, the large number of pages in a school dictionary can make it a difficult and time-consuming exercise for children trying to locate the many words they wish to spell when writing. *Spell It Yourself*, with far fewer pages, has been compiled specially to help children quickly and easily locate the words, without the distraction of occasionally complicated definitions found in a dictionary.

Clearly, children are likely to learn to spell correctly words which they are anxious to use in their own writing. In free writing, children are often not content to misspell, if they can avoid it; and they may waste much time, at the expense of the content of their written work, trying to discover the correct spelling of words they need. The usual school spelling books of groups of words for memorization, children's own word books, and most junior dictionaries cannot give proper guidance. The teacher often has little time to help with individual problems. It is hoped that this book, *Spell It Yourself*, will provide a useful tool, easy for children to handle for themselves as they need.

Spelling – with the exception of a limited number of the commonest words – seems a subject for individual learning: no two children wish to make use of exactly the same words in their written expression. This reference list, of nearly 7,500 root words, reflects those used most frequently in upper primary as well as lower secondary classes; but the list also includes many of the less common words which individual children may need.

Children's ability to read and recognize words is much greater than their ability to spell them; in this book they should be able quickly to find and identify the words they hesitate to spell. The order of the words is alphabetical, and if a child knows the first two letters – as he or she usually does – of the word required, the child can find in the **Index** the number of the page where he or she should look for it.

The alphabetical basis of the book provides useful training in the use of a dictionary. Word derivatives are usually shown by suffixes to the right of the columns which need only be added to the root words (see the **Instructions**).

In general, children learn best by finding out for themselves. In this book they will learn to look up words for themselves and to spell them correctly the first time, instead of making mistakes which have later to be corrected. They will steadily increase their written vocabulary, becoming more 'word-conscious' all the time. With this book at their elbow, and under the direction of a teacher aware of its purpose, they will be teaching themselves how to spell.

G.T. Hawker

Instructions

1. Think hard about the word you wish to spell and try to decide with which two letters it starts.
2. Find these two letters in the Index and you will see the number of the page where the word can be found or where you should begin looking for it.
3. Turn to this page and look down the column under these two letters until you find the word you want.

Many of the words you will wish to write are known as compound words (having two or more parts) and are either joined (eg motorbike), separated (eg motor car) or hyphenated (eg half-term). The examples underneath show how these are indicated in the book.

It may be necessary to add the word endings shown in *italics* on the right-hand side of the column in order to build up the complete word you want, eg

rich   *er, est, ly, ness, es*

tea   *cake, cup, pot, time, s*

Here the words **richer, richest, richly, richness** and **riches** may be built up, and also **teacake(s), teacup(s), teapot(s), teatime(s)** and **teas**.

Where a slash (/) is in front of an *italic* word, eg

tea   */bags, /chest, /shop, /towel, s*

this means the words are written separately, eg

tea bag(s), tea chest(s), tea shop(s), tea towel(s).

Where a hyphen (-) is in front of an *italic* word, eg

half   *-price, -term, -time*

This means that the two words are joined by the hyphen, eg

half-price, half-term, half-time.

Where the last letter or letters of a word are in *italics* these must be left off before adding to the other endings, eg

happ*y*   *ier, iest, ily, iness*

Here the *y* must be left off before making:

happier, happiest, happily, happiness.

The plurals of most nouns may be formed by adding the letter, or letters, shown in *italics* on the extreme right of the column. A few nouns have their plurals given in full on the right of the column, and you will notice that some nouns have two plurals, either of which may be used, eg **cactuses** or **cacti, hoofs** or **hooves, fish** or **fishes**.

All the words with *ed, ing* after them are verbs or may be used as verbs. If you require the word to end in either *ed* or *ing*, remember the following:

(a) **kick**   *ed, ing, s*   =   **kicked**   **kicking**   **kicks**

Here *ed* or *ing* or *s* may be added to the verb without changing the word at all.

(b) **stab**   *bed, bing, s*   =   **stabbed**   **stabbing**   **stabs**

   stop   *ped, ping, s*   =   **stopped**   **stopping**   **stops**

Here you can see that the final consonant (the last letter) of these verbs has to be doubled before adding *ed* or *ing*.

(c) **blame**   *d, ¢ing, s*   =   **blamed**   **blaming**   **blames**

Where a verb ends in a letter **e** the *d* or *s* may be added to the word but the **e** must be dropped before adding *ing*. An *¢* is placed before the *ing* to remind you of this.

There are a few other verbs which change their endings in different ways. You will usually find these endings printed by the side of, above or below, the verb, eg

began		**lie**	*d, s*	**carry**	*ing*
begin	*ning, s*	**lying**		**carr**ied	*ies*
begun					

Warning: A word which has a star (*) after it has the same sound, or almost the same sound, as another word, but it has a different meaning and spelling, eg **knew* new*; their* there* they're*; which* witch***. The word endings will help you to decide which of these words you want and so will the words in brackets. These are included to guide you; they are not always exact definitions. The words are paired in small print at the bottom of the page. If you find that you have looked up the wrong word you may easily see how the other is spelt and where it may be found in its correct alphabetical place in the book.

The alphabet

There are 26 letters in the alphabet:

a	b	c	d	e	f	g	h	i	j	k	l	m
A	B	C	D	E	F	G	H	I	J	K	L	M

n	o	p	q	r	s	t	u	v	w	x	y	z
N	O	P	Q	R	S	T	U	V	W	X	Y	Z

Vowel: This is the name given to any one of the five letters a e i o u – underlined above.

Consonant: This is the name given to any one of the other twenty-one letters in the alphabet.

Parts of speech

Noun: A naming word, eg *boy, man, cat, house, Susan, England.*
On *Monday John* went by *coach* to *London Zoo* with his *teacher, Mr. Smith,* and other *children* from his *class.*

Pronoun: A word used instead of a noun, eg *me, she, it, we, us, him.*
You and *I* will go now and *he* can come later with *them.*

Adjective: A word that is 'added to' a noun to describe it, eg *fat, thin, big, brown, green, ugly, pretty, delicious.*
A *funny, little, old* man with a *large* nose and a *grey* beard showed the *small* children his *beautiful* garden.

Verb: A doing word; a word that tells what is done, eg *do, go, stay, talk, shout, jump, lift, fight, eat, drink.*
Stop running or you will *fall* and *hurt* yourself.

Adverb: A word that tells how, when or where something happens, eg *soon, often, there, now, never, quickly, carefully, carelessly.*
Yesterday when I came *here* I jumped *over* that wall.

Preposition: A word that is placed before a noun, eg *by, in, into, at, for, under, over, against, near.*
Alisha went *with* her sister *on* a bus *to* the town.

Conjunction: A word that joins sentences, phrases or words, eg *or, than, though, although, because, while, unless.*
Ben *and* Caitlin will go *if* it is fine *but* not *if* it rains.

Interjection: A word used as an exclamation, eg *Ah! Alas! Hey!*
Oh! You did frighten me. *Ouch!* That hurt.

Article: One of the three words *a, an* or *the.*
A boy rode on *an* elephant at *the* zoo.

ab

aback	
abandon	ed, ing, ment, s
abate	d, ǿing, ment, s
abbey	s
abbot	s
abduct	ed, ing, ion, s
abhor	red, ring, rence, rent, s
abide	d, ǿing, s
abilit y	ies
ablaze	
able	r, st, -bodied
abnormal	ity, ly
aboard	
abolish	ed, ing, es
abominable	
abominate	d, ǿing, ǿion, s
Aborigine	Aboriginals
abound	ed, ing, s
about	
above	/board
abreast	
abroad	
abrupt	ly, ness
abscess	es
abseil	ed, ing, s
absence	s
absent	-minded, ly, ee, s
absolute	ly
absorb	ed, ing, ent, tion, s
abstain	ed, ing, s
absurd	ity, ly
abundance	
abundant	ly
abuse	d, ǿing, ǿive, s
abysmal	ly
abyss	es

ac

academ y	ies
accelerate	d, ǿing, ǿion, ǿor, s
accent	s
accept* (receive)	able, ed, ing, s
access	ible
accessor y	ies
accident	al, ally, s
accommodate	d, ǿing, ǿion, s
accompany	ing
accompan ied	ies
accomplish	ed, ing, es
according	ly
account	ed, ing, able, ant, s
accumulate	d, ǿing, ǿion, s
accuracy	
accurate	ly
accuse	d, ǿing, ǿation, s
accustom	ed, ing, s
ache	d, ǿing, s
achieve	d, ǿing, ment, s
acid	ic, ity, /rain, s
acknowledge	d, ǿing, ment, s
acorn	s
acquaint	ed, ing, ance, s
acquire	d, ǿing, s
acquit	ted, ting, tal, s
acre	age, s
acrobat	ic, s
across	
act	ed, ing, or, s
actress	es
action	s
active	ly
activit y	ies
actual	ly
acute	ly, ness

* accept
except

ad

adapt	able, ed, ing, or, s
add	ed, ing, s
addict	ed, ion, ive, s
adder	s
addition	al, s
address	ed, ing, es
adequate	ly
adhere	d, ∅ing, s
adhesive	s
adjacent	
adjective	s
adjoin	ed, ing, s
adjust	able, ed, ing, ment, s
admirable	∅y
admiral	s
admiration	
admire	d, ∅ing, r, s
admission	s
admit	ted, ting, tance, s
adopt	ed, ing, ion, s
adore	d, ∅ing, ∅able, s
adorn	ed, ing, ment, s
adrift	
adult	s
advance	d, ∅ing, ment, s
advantage	ous, s
adventure	r, s
adventurous	ly, ness
adverb	s
adversar y	ies
advertise	d, ∅ing, r, s
advertisement	s
advice	
advisable	
advise	d, ∅ing, r, s
advocate	d, ∅ing, s

ae

aerial	s
aerodrome	s
aeronaut	ic, s
aeroplane	s
aerosol	/can, s

af

affair	s
affect	ed, ing, s
affection	s
affectionate	ly
affix	ed, ing, es
afford	ed, ing, able, s
afloat	
afraid	
after	
afternoon	s
afterwards	

ag

again	
against	
age	d, less, /group, /range, s
ageing or aging	
agent	s
aggravate	d, ∅ing, ∅ion, s
aggressive	ly, ness
aghast	
agile	ly
agilit y	ies
agitate	d, ∅ing, ∅ion, s
ago	
agonize	d, ∅ing, s
agon y	ies
agree	able, d, ing, ment, s

agriculture &al

aground

ai

aid	ed, ing, s
ail* (be ill)	ed, ing, ment, s
aim	ed, ing, less, lessly, s
air*	ed, ing, crew, mail, tight
air*	field, gun, line, port, strip, way, s
air*	man, men, woman, women
aircraft	/carrier
air force	s
air y	ier, iest, ily, iness
aisle* (space between rows of seats)	s

al

alarm	ed, ing, ist, /bell, /clock, s
album	s
alcohol	ism, ic, s
alcove	s
ale* (beer)	s
alert	ed, ing, ly, ness, s
algebra	
alibi	s
alien	s
alight	ed, ing, s
alike	
alive	
allerg y	ic, ies
alley	way, s
alligator	s
allot	ted, ting, ment, s
allow (let)	ed*, ing, ance, s
all right	
all y	ies
almond	/paste, /tree, s

almost	
alone	
along	side
aloud* (not quietly)	
alphabet	ical, ically, s
already	
Alsatian	s
also	
altar* (church table)	s
alter* (change)	ed, ing, ation, s
alternate	d, &ing, ly, s
alternative	ly, s
although	
altitude	s
altogether	
aluminium	
always	

am

amateur	ish, s
amaze	d, &ing, ment, s
amber	
ambition	s
ambitious	ly
amble	d, &ing, s
ambulance	man, men, woman, women, s
ambush	ed, ing, es
amend	ed, ing, ment, s
amiable	&y
amid or amidst	
amiss	
ammunition	
among or amongst	
amount	ed, ing, s
amphibian	s
amphibious	ly
ample	r, st, &y, ness

*	ail	air	aisle	allowed	* altar
	ale	heir	I'll	aloud	alter
			isle		

amplifier	s		anvil	s
amputate	d, ∅ing, ∅ion, s		anxiety	ies
amuse	d, ∅ing, ment, s		anxious	ly
			any	body, one, how, thing, way, where

an

anaesthetic	s			
analyse	d, ∅ing, ∅is, s		apart	
ancestor	s		apartment	s
ancestry	ies		ape	d, ∅ing, s
anchor	ed, ing, age, s		apiece	
ancient	s		apologetic	ally
anemone	s		apologize	d, ∅ing, s
angel	ic, s		apology	ies
anger	ed, ing, s		apostle	s
angry	ier, iest, ily		appal	led, ling, lingly, s
angle	d, ∅ing, r, s		apparatus	es or apparatus
anguish	ed, ing, es		apparent	ly
animal	s		appeal	ed, ing, ingly, s
ankle	-bone, -deep, /sock, s		appear	ed, ing, ance, s
annihilate	d, ∅ing, ∅ion, s		appendicitis	
anniversary	ies		appetite	s
announce	d, ∅ing, r, ment, s		appetizing	ly
annoy	ed, ing, ance, s		applaud	ed, ing, s
annual	ly, s		applause	
anoint	ed, ing, ment, s		apple	/juice, /pie, /sauce, /tart, /tree, s
anonymous	ly		appliance	s
anorak	s		applicable	
another			applicant	s
answer	ed, ing, able, phone, s		application	s
ant	eater, hill, s		apply	ing
Antarctic or Antartica			applied	ies
antelope	s		appoint	ed, ing, ment, s
anticipate	d, ∅ing, ∅ion, s		appreciate	d, ∅ing, ∅ion, ∅ive, s
antics			apprehension	s
antique	s		apprentice	d, ∅ing, ship, s
antiseptic	s		approach	ed, ing, able, es
antler	s		appropriate	ly

ap

approve	d, ⌀ing, ⌀al, s
approximate	ly, d, ⌀ing, s
apricot	s
April	/fool, s
apron	s

aq

aquarium	s or aquaria
aquatic	s
aqueduct	s

ar

Arab	ian, ic, s
arable	
arc* (curve)	/lamp, /light, s
arcade	s
arch	ed, ing, es
archway	s
archaeological	ly
archaeologist	s
archaeology	
archer	y, s
architect	ure, ural, s
Arctic	
are	
aren't (are not)	
area	s
arena	s
argue	d, ⌀ing, s
argument	ative, s
arise	n, ⌀ing, s
arithmetic	al
ark* (boat)	s
arm	ed, ing, band, chair, ful, hole, pit, s
armada	s
armistice	s
armour	ed, y, -plated, -plating
army	ies
arose	
around	
arouse	d, ⌀ing, s
arrange	d, ⌀ing, r, ment, s
array	ed, ing, s
arrest	ed, ing, s
arrive	d, ⌀ing, ⌀al, s
arrow	head, s
arsenic	
art	/school, /teacher, work, s
artist	ic, ically, s
artful	ly, ness
artery	ies
article	s
artificial	ity, ly
artillery	man, /officer, /regiment

as

ascend	ed, ing, s
ascent	s
ascertain	ed, ing, s
ash	en, y, es
ashamed	
ashore	
aside	
ask	ed, ing, s
asleep	
asparagus	
asphyxiate	d, ⌀ing, ⌀ion, s
aspirin	s
assail	ed, ing, ant, s
assassin	ation, s
assassinate	d, ⌀ing, s
assault	ed, ing, s
assemble	d, ⌀ing, s

* arc
   ark

assembl y	ies
asset	s
assign	ed, ing, ment, s
assist	ed, ing, ance, ant, s
associate	d, ∅ing, ∅ion, s
assort	ed, ment, s
assume	d, ∅ing, s
assumption	s
assure	d, ∅ing, ∅ance, s
aster	s
asthma	tic
astonish	ed, ing, ment, es
astound	ed, ing, s
astray	
astride	
astrologer	s
astrolog y	ical
astronaut	s
astronomer	s
astronom y	ical
asylum	/seeker, s

at

ate* (eat)	
athlete	s
athletic	ally, s
Atlantic	
atlas	es
atmosphere	s
atom	ic, /bomb, s
atrocious	ly, ness
atrocit y	ies
attach	ed, ing, able, es
attachment	s
attack	ed, ing, er, s
attain	ed, ing, able, ment, s
attempt	ed, ing, s

attend	ed, ing, ance, ant, s
attention	s
attentive	ly, ness
attic	s
attitude	s
attract	ed, ing, ion, s
attractive	ly, ness
attribute	d, ∅ing, s

au

auburn	
auction	ed, ing, eer, /room, s
audible	
audience	s
audition	ed, ing, s
August	s
aunt	s
auntie or **aunty**	**aunties**
au pair	s
author	s
authorit y	ies
authorize	d, ∅ing, ∅ation, s
autobiograph y	ical, ies
autograph	ed, ing, s
automatic	ally
automation	
autumn	al, s

av

available	
avalanche	s
avenge	d, ∅ing, r, s
avenue	s
average	d, ∅ing, s
avert	ed, ing, s
aviar y	ies

* ate
* eight (8)

aviation	
avocado	s
avoid	ed, ing, able, ance, s

aw

await	ed, ing, s
awake	✊ing, s
awaken	ed, ing, s
award	ed, ing, s
aware	ness
away	
awe	-inspiring, some, -struck
awful	ly, ness
awhile	
awkward	ly, ness
awning	s
awoke	n
awry	

ax

axe	d, ✊ing, /blade, /handle, s
ax is	es
axle	s

ba

babble	d, ✊ing, r, s
baboon	s
bab y	ies
bachelor	s
back	ed, ing, cloth, ground, log, yard, s
backward	ness, s
bacon	
bad	-tempered, ly, ness
badge	s
badger	ed, ing, s
badminton	/court, /player, /racket

baffle	d, ✊ing, s
bag	ged, ging, ful, -snatcher, s
baggage	
bagg y	ier, iest, ily, iness
bagpipes	
bail* (wicket cross-piece)	s
bail* or **bale** (escape)	ed, ing, er, s
bait	ed, ing, s
bake	d, ✊ing, r, s
baked beans	
baker y	ies
balance	d, ✊ing, r, s
balcon y	ies
bald	ing, er, est, ness, -headed
bale* (bundle)	d, ✊ing, r, s
bale* or **bail** (escape)	d, ✊ing, r, s
ball*	/game, point, room, s
ballast	
ballerina	s
ballet	/dancing, /dancer, /shoe, s
balloon	ist, s
ballot	ed, ing, /paper, s
bamboo	s
ban	ned, ning, s
banana	/skin, s
band	ed, ing, sman, smen, stand, s
bandage	d, ✊ing, s
bandit	s
bang	ed, ing, er, s
bangle	s
banish	ed, ing, es, ment
banister	s
banjo	ist, s
bank	ed, ing, er, /book, /card, note, s
bankrupt	ed, ing, s, cy
banner	s
banoffee	/pie

	bail	ball
*	bale	bawl

banquet	*ed, ing, s*	bathe		*d, ∅ing, r, s*
bantam	*s*	baton* (a short stick)		*s*
baptism	*s*	battalion		*s*
baptize	*d, ∅ing, s*	batten* (a flat strip of wood)		*ed, ing, s*
bar	*red, ring, man, maid, tender, s*	batter		*ed, ing, s*
barbecue	*d, ∅ing, s*	batter *y*		*ies*
barbed	*/wire*	battle		*d, ∅ing, axe, field, ship, s*
barber	*s*	bawl* (shout; cry out)		*ed, ing, s*
bare* (naked; empty)	*ly, ness, d, ∅ing, s*	bay		*/window, s*
bargain	*ed, ing, er, /hunter, s*	bayonet		*ed, ing, s*
barge	*d, ∅ing, e, pole, s*	bazaar		*s*
bark	*ed, ing, er, s*			
barley	*corn, /sugar, /water, s*	**be**		
barn	*/dance, /owl, yard, s*	beach* (seashore)		*es*
barnacle	*s*	beacon		*s*
barometer	*s*	bead		*ed, ing, work, s*
baron* (lord)	*et, s*	beak		*s*
barracks		beaker		*s*
barrel	*ful, s*	beam		*ed, ing, s*
barren* (bare; empty)	*ness*	bean* (plant)		*bag, pole, stalk, s*
barricade	*d, ∅ing, s*	bear* (carry; endure)		*able, ing, er, s*
barrier	*s*	bear* (animal)		*skin, s*
barrister	*s*	beard		*ed, s*
barrow	*/boy, s*	beast		*s*
barter	*ed, ing, er, s*	beastl *y*		*ier, iest, iness*
base	*d, ∅ing, r, st, ly, less, ness, line, s*	beat* (hit; defeat)		*en, ing, er, s*
baseball	*/bat, /cap, /player, /team, s*	beautiful		*ly*
basement	*s*	beaut *y*		*ies*
bash	*ed, ing, es*	beaver		*s*
bashful	*ly, ness*	became		
basin	*ful, s*	because		
bask	*ed, ing, s*	beckon		*ed, ing, s*
basket	*ball, ful, s*	become		*∅ing, s*
bat	*ted, ting, s*	bed *ded, ding, clothes, side, time, room, s*		
bat	*sman, smen, swoman, swomen*	bee		*hive, line, keeper, s*
batch	*es*	beech* (tree)		*es*
bath	*ed, ing, mat, robe, room, /water, s*	beef		*burger, eater, steak, s*

been* (past of be)	
beer	y, /barrel, /bottle, /can, s
beet* (vegetable)	root, s
beetle	s
before	hand
beg	ged, ging, gar, s
began	
begin	ning, ner, s
begun	
begrudge	d, ∅ing, s
behave	d, ∅ing, ∅iour, s
behead	ed, ing, s
behind	hand
being	s
belief	s
believe	d, ∅ing, r, s
bell	-ringer, /tower, s
bellow	ed, ing, er, s
belong	ed, ing, s
below	
belt	ed, ing, s
bench	es
bend	ing, er, s
bent	
beneath	
beneficial	ly
benefit	ed, ing, s
benevolent	ly
beret* (cap)	s
berry* (fruit)	ies
berserk	
berth* (bunk; ship's moorings)	ed, ing, s
beside	s
besiege	d, ∅ing, r, s
best	-known, -seller
bet	ted, ting, ter, s
betray	al, ed, ing, er, s

better	ed, ing, s
between	
beware	
bewilder	ed, ing, ment, s
beyond	

bi

Bible	s
bicker	ed, ing, s
bicycle	/chain, /clip, /pump, s
bid	ding, der, s
bide	d, ∅ing, s
big	ger, gest, ness
bike	d, ∅ing, r, /ride, /shed, s
bikini	s
bilberry	ies
bilge	/water, /pump, s
bilious	ness
bill	s
billet	ed, ing, s
billiards	
billion	s
billow	ed, ing, s
bind	ing, er, s
bingo	/hall, /player, s
binoculars	
biography	ical, ies
biology	ical, ist
biped	s
birch	es
bird	/bath, cage, seed, song, /table, s
birth* (born)	mark, place, /rate, s
birthday	/card, /cake, /present, s
biscuit	/tin, s
bisect	ed, ing, ion, s
bishop	s
bison	bison

---

* been · beet · beret · berth
  bean · beat · berry · birth
  ·   ·   · bury

bit	*ty, s*
bitch	*es*
bite	*∅ing, r, s*
bitten	
bitter	*er, est, ly, ness*

bl

black	*ed, ing, er, est, ness, smith, s*
black	*-beetle, bird, board, currant, s*
blackberr *y*	*ies*
blacken	*ed, ing, s*
blackmail	*ed, ing, er, s*
blade	*d, s*
blame	*d, ∅ing, less, s*
blancmange	*s*
blank	*ed, ing, ly, ness, s*
blanket	*s*
blare	*d, ∅ing, s*
blast	*ed, ing, s*
blaze	*d, ∅ing, s*
blazer	*s*
bleach	*ed, ing, es*
bleak	*er, est, ly, ness*
blear *y*	*ier, iest, ily, iness*
bleat	*ed, ing, s*
bleed	*ing, s*
bled	
blend	*ed, ing, er, s*
bless	*ed, ing, ings, es*
blew* (blow)	
blind	*ed, ing, ly, ness, s*
blind man's buff	
blindfold	*ed, ing, s*
blink	*ed, ing, er, s*
blister	*ed, ing, s*
blizzard	*s*
block	*age, ed, ing, s*

blockade	*d, ∅ing, s*
blog	*ged, ging, ger, s*
blond (male)	*/hair, s*
blonde (female)	*/hair, s*
blood	*hound, shed, stained, thirsty, y*
bloom	*ed, ing, s*
blossom	*ed, ing, s*
blot	*ted, ting, ter, s*
blouse	*s*
blow	*n, ing, y, er, lamp, pipe, s*
blue* (colour)	*r, st, ness, bell, bottle, s*
blunder	*ed, ing, s*
blunt	*ed, ing, er, est, ly, ness, s*
blush	*ed, ing, es*
bluster	*ed, ing, y, s*

bo

boar* (male pig)	*s*
board* (wood; enter; lodge)	*ed, ing, s*
boarder* (one who boards; lodger)	*s*
boast	*ed, ing, er, s*
boastful	*ly, ness*
boat	*ing, er, /race, yard, s*
bob	*bed, bing, sleigh, s*
bod *y*	*ies*
bog	*gy, s*
boil	*ed, ing, er, s*
boisterous	*ly, ness*
bold	*er*, est, ly, ness*
bolt	*ed, ing, -hole, s*
bomb	*ed, ing, er, proof, shell, sight, s*
bombard	*ed, ing, ment, s*
bone	*d, ∅ing, ∅y, /dry, /idle, shaker, s*
bonfire	*s*
bonnet	*s*
bonn *y*	*ier, iest, iness*
bonus	*es*

---

book	ed, ing, case, let, shop, seller, s
booking office	s
boom	ed, ing, s
boot	ed, ing, lace, s
border* (edge)	ed, ing, line, s
bore* (drill hole; weary)	d*, ∅ing, dom, s
born* (birth)	
borne* (carried)	
borrow	ed, ing, er, s
boss	ed, ing, es
boss y	ier, iest, ily, iness
botan y	ical, ist
both	
bother	ed, ing, some, s
bottle	d, ∅ing, ful, neck, s
bottom	less, s
bough* (branch)	s
bought (buy)	
boulder* (large rock)	s
bounce	d, ∅ing, ∅y, r, s
bound	ed, ing, less, s
boundar y	ies
bouquet	s
bow* (bend)	ed, ing, s
bow	man, men, shot, string, -tie, s
bowl (cricket, etc)	ed, ing, er, s
bowl (round dish)	ful, s
box	ed, ing, es
boxer	s
Boxing Day	s
boy* (lad)	ish, hood, friend, s
Boy Scout	s

br

brace	d, ∅ing, s
bracelet	s
bracken	
bracket	ed, ing, s
brag	ged, ging, gart, s
braid	ed, ing, s
brain	ed, ing, less, storm, wave, s
brain y	ier, iest, ily, iness
brake* (to stop)	d, ∅ing, s
bramble	s
branch	ed, ing, es
brand	ed, ing, /new, s
brandish	ed, ing, es
brand y	ies
brass	es
brave	d, ∅ing, r, ry, st, ly, s
bravo	s
brawl	ed, ing, er, s
brawn	
brawn y	ier, iest, iness
brazen	ed, ing, ly, ness
brazier	s
bread*	/bin, board, /sauce, crumb, /roll, s
breadth	s
break*	able, age, ing, er, -down, water, s
breakfast	ed, ing, s
breast	plate, stroke, s
breath	less, lessly, taking, s
breathe	d, ∅ing, r, s
bred* (brought-up)	
breed	ing, er, s
breeze	s
breez y	ier, iest, ily, iness
brevity	
brew	ed, ing, er, s
brewer y	ies
bribe	d, ∅ing, ry, s
brick	ed, ing, laying, layer, work, yard, s
bridal* (of a bride, wedding)	/gown
bride	groom, smaid, s

---

border	bore	born	bough	boulder	boy	brake	bread	bridal
boarder	boar	borne	bow	bolder	buoy	break	bred	bridle

*

bridge	s
bridle* (horse's headgear)	/path, way, s
brief	ed, ing, er, est, ly, ness, case, s
brigade	s
brigand	s
bright	er, est, ly, ness
brighten	ed, ing, s
brilliance	
brilliant	ly
brim	med, ming, ful, s
bring	ing, s
brink	s
brisk	er, est, ly, ness
bristle	d, ∅ing, ∅y, s
brittle	ness
broad	er, est, ly, -minded, side, s
broaden	ed, ing, s
broadcast	ing, er, s
brocade	s
broccoli	
brochure	s
broke	
broken	-down, -hearted
bronchitis	
bronze	d, ∅ing, s
brooch	es
brood	ed, ing, y, s
brook	s
broom	stick, s
broth	s
brother	ly, s
brother (s)**-in-law**	
brought (bring)	
brown	ed, ing, er, est, ish, ness, s
brownie (small cake)	s
Brownie Guide	s
bruise	d, ∅ing, r, s

brunette	s
brush	ed, ing, es
Brussels sprout	s
brutal	ity, ly
brute	s

bu

bubble	d, ∅ing, /bath, gum, s
bubbl y	ier, iest, iness
buccaneer	s
buck	ed, ing, s
bucket	ful, s
buckle	d, ∅ing, s
bud	ded, ding, s
budge	d, ∅ing, s
budgerigar	s
budget	ed, ing, s
buffalo	es or **buffalo**
buffer	s
buffet (blow)	ed, ing, s
buffet (meal)	s
bugle	/call, r, s
build	ing, er, s
built	
bulb	s
bulge	d, ∅ing, s
bulk	
bulk y	ier, iest, ily, iness
bull	dog, fight, frog, ring, -terrier, s
bull's-eye	s
bulldoze	d, ∅ing, r, s
bullet	/hole, proof, /wound, s
bulletin	s
bullion	
bullock	s
bully	ing
bull ied	ies

---

* bridle
bridal

bulrush	*es*
bumble-bee	*s*
bump	*ed, ing, er, s*
bump *y*	*ier, iest, ily, iness*
bunch	*ed, ing, es*
bundle	*d, ∉ing, s*
bung	*ed, ing, -hole, s*
bungalow	*s*
bungle	*d, ∉ing, r, s*
bunk	*/bed, s*
bunker	*ed, ing, s*
Bunsen burner	*s*
bunting	
buoy* (floating marker)	*ant, ed, ing, s*
burden	*ed, ing, some, s*
bureau	*x* or *s*
burglar	*/alarm, s*
burglar *y*	*ies*
burgle	*d, ∉ing, s*
burial	*/ground, /place, s*
burl *y*	*ier, iest, iness*
burn	*ed, ing, er, s*
burnt or **burned**	
burrow	*ed, ing, er, s*
burst	*ing, s*
bury* (put under ground)	*ing*
bur *ied*	*ies*
bus	*es, sed, sing, /driver, /stop*
busb *y*	*ies*
bush	*es*
bush *y*	*ier, iest, ily, iness*
business	*man, men, woman, women, es*
bustle	*d, ∉ing, r, s*
busy	*body, ing, ness*
bus *ied*	*ier, iest, ily, ies*
butcher	*ed, ing, s*
butler	*s*

butter	*ed, ing, scotch, cup, s*
butterfl *y*	*ies*
button	*ed, ing, hole, s*
buy* (purchase)	*ing, er, s*
buzz	*ed, ing, es*
buzzer	*s*
buzzard	*s*

by

by* (near to, etc)	
bye* (a run scored in cricket; goodbye)	*s*
bygone	*s*
bypass	*ed, ing, es*
bystander	*s*
byway	*s*

ca

cabaret	*s*
cabbage	*s*
cabin	*/boy, /crew, s*
cabinet	*/maker, s*
cable	*d, ∉ing, gram, /car, s*
cackle	*d, ∉ing, r, s*
cactus	*es* or **cacti**
caddie* (golfer's club-carrier)	*d, s*
caddying	
cadd *y** (tea box)	*ies*
cadet	*s*
cadge	*d, ∉ing, r, s*
café	*s*
cafeteria	*s*
cage	*d, ∉ing, s*
cake	*d, ∉ing, s*
calamit *y*	*ies*
calculate	*d, ∉ing, ∉ion, ∉or, s*
calendar	*s*

*	buoy	bury	*	buy	caddie
	boy	beret		by	caddy
		berry		bye	

calf	*skin,* **calves**	**car**	*load, /park, port, s*
call	*ed, ing, er, s*	**caramel**	*s*
callous	*ly, ness*	**caravan**	*ning, ner, /site, s*
calm	*ed, ing, er, est, ly, ness, s*	**carcass**	*es*
camcorder	*s*	**card**	*board, /game, /player, /table, s*
came		**cardigan**	*s*
camel	*s*	**cardinal**	*/number, s*
camera	*man, men, s*	**care**	*d, ∅ing, r, free, taker, s*
camouflage	*d, ∅ing, s*	**careful**	*ly, ness*
camp	*ed, ing, er, /bed, fire, site, s*	**careless**	*ly, ness*
campaign	*ed, ing, er, s*	**career**	*ed, ing, s*
canal	*/boat, s*	**caress**	*ed, ing, es*
canary	*ies*	**cargo**	*es*
cancel	*led, ling, lation, s*	**caricature**	*d, ∅ing, s*
candidate	*s*	**carnation**	*s*
candle	*light, lit, wick, stick, s*	**carnival**	*s*
candy	*ied, ies*	**carnivore**	*∅ous*
cane	*d, ∅ing, s*	**carol**	*led, ling, ler, /service, /singer, s*
cannibal	*ism, s*	**carpenter**	*s*
cannon	*/ball, /fire, /shot, s or* **cannon**	**carpentry**	
cannot		**carpet**	*ed, ing, /sweeper, s*
can't (cannot)		**carriage**	*way, s*
canoe	*d, ing, ist, s*	**carrot**	*s*
canteen	*s*	**carry**	*ing*
canter	*ed, ing, s*	**carr**ied	*ies*
canvas* (strong cloth)	*es*	**carrier**	*/bag, /pigeon, s*
canvass* (seek votes, orders)	*ed, ing, es*	**cart**	*ed, ing, load, horse, wheel, s*
canyon	*s*	**carton**	*s*
capable	*∅y*	**cartoon**	*ist, s*
cape	*s*	**cartridge**	*/belt, /case, s*
capital	*s*	**carve**	*d, ∅ing, r, s*
capsize	*d, ∅ing, s*	**cascade**	*d, ∅ing, s*
capsule	*s*	**case**	*s*
captain	*ed, ing, s*	**cash**	*ed, ing, /box, es*
captive	*s*	**cashier**	*s*
captivity		**cask**	*et, s*
capture	*d, ∅ing, s*	**casserole**	*d, ∅ing, s*

---

* canvas
canvass

ce ch

cassette	/player, /recorder, s
cast	ing, away, s
castanet	s
castle	s
casual	ly, ness, s
casualt y	ies
catalogue	d, ǿing, s
catamaran	s
catapult	ed, ing, s
catastrophe	s
catch	ing, es
catch y	ier, iest, iness
categor y	ies
cater	ed, ing, er, s
caterpillar	s
cathedral	s
Catherine wheel	s
Catholic	s
catkin	s
cattle	/market, /shed, /show, /truck
caught* (catch)	
cauldron	s
cauliflower	s
cause	d, ǿing, s
caution	ed, ing, s
cautious	ly, ness
Cavalier	s
cavalry	man, men, /officer
cave	d, ǿing, man, men, /dweller, s
cavern	s
cavit y	ies

ce

cease	d, ǿing, less, lessly, s
cedar	wood, /tree, s
ceiling* (roof of room)	s
celandine	s

celebrate	d, ǿing, ǿion, s
celebrit y	ies
celery	
cell* (small room)	s
cellar* (underground room)	s
cellist	s
cello	s
cellophane	
cement	ed, ing, /mixer, s
cemeter y	ies
census	es
cent* (coin)	s
centigrade	
centimetre	s
central	/heating, ly
centre	d, ǿing, /forward, piece, s
centur y	ies
cereal* (wheat, oats, etc)	s
ceremon y	ies
certain	ly, ty
certificate	s
certif y	ied, s

ch

chaffinch	es
chain	ed, ing, /mail, saw, /store, s
chair	ed, ing, man, woman, lift, s
chalet	s
chalk	ed, ing, y, s
challenge	d, ǿing, r, s
chamber	s
chamois	/leather
champagne	/bottle, /cork, s
champion	ed, ing, ship, s
chance	d, ǿing, s
chandelier	s
change	able, d, ǿing, s

---

* caught	ceiling		
court	sealing		

*	cell	cellar	cent	cereal
	sell	seller	scent	serial
			sent	

channel	led, ling, /swimmer, s	**chemist**	s
chant	ed, ing, s	**chemistry**	
Chanukah or **Hanukkah**		**cheque*** (money-order)	book, s
chaos		**cherish**	ed, ing, es
chaotic	ally	**cherr**y	ies
chapel	s	**chess**	board, /piece, /player, set
chapter	s	**chest**	s
char	red, ring, woman, women, s	**chestnut**	/tree, s
character	istic, s	**chew**	ed, ing, y, er, s
charade	s	**chewing gum**	
charcoal		**chick**	weed, s
charge	d, ¢ing, r, s	**chicken**	/feed, /wire, s or **chicken**
chariot	eer, s	**chickenpox**	
charity	ies	**chief**	ly, tain, s
charm	ed, ing, er, s	**chilblain**	s
chart	ed, ing, s	**child**	ish, hood, like, less, **children**
chase	d, ¢ing, r, s	**chill**	ed, ing, er, s
chasm	s	**chill**y	ier, iest, ily, iness
chat	ted, ting, s	**chime**	d, ¢ing, s
chatter	ed, ing, er, s	**chimney**	/pot, /stack, /sweep, s
chatty	ier, iest, ily, iness	**chimpanzee**	s
chauffeur	s	**chin**	strap, s
cheap* (not dear)	er, est, ly, ness	**china**	ware
cheapen	ed, ing, s	**chink**	ed, ing, s
cheat	ed, ing, er, s	**chintz**	es
check*	ed, ing, er, list, out, point, -up, s	**chip**	ped, ping, per, s
check* (pattern)	ed, s	**chirp**	ed, ing, s
cheek	ed, ing, bone, s	**chirp**y	ier, iest, ily, iness
cheeky	ier, iest, ily, iness	**chisel**	led, ling, s
cheep* (bird sound)	ed, ing, s	**chivalrous**	ly
cheer	ed, ing, leader, s	**chivalry**	
cheerful	ly, ness	**chlorine**	
cheerless	ly, ness	**chloroform**	ed, ing, s
cheery	ier, iest, ily, iness	**chocolate**	/biscuit, s
cheese	burger, cake, cloth, /straw, s	**choice**	r, st, ly, ness, s
chef	s	**choir*** (of singers)	boy, girl, master, s
chemical	ly, s	**choke**	d, ¢ing, s

---

choose	ɇing, s
chose	n
chop	ped, ping, per, s
choppy	ier, iest, ily, iness
chopstick	s
chorus	ed, ing, es
Christ	
christen	ed, ing, s
Christian	ity, /name, s
Christmas	/box, es, /card, /gift /tree, sy
chromium	-plated, -plating
chronic	ally
chronological	ly
chrysalis	es
chrysanthemum	s
chubb y	ier, iest, ily, iness
chuckle	d, ɇing, s
chug	ged, ging, s
chum	med, ming, s
chumm y	ier, iest, ily, iness
chunk	s
church	es
churchyard	s
churn	ed, ing, s
chute* (a slide)	s
chutney	s

ci

cider	s
cigar	/smoker, s
cigarette	/end, /case, /packet, /lighter, s
cinder	s
cinema	-goer, /ticket, s
circle	d, ɇing, s
circular	s
circulate	d, ɇing, ɇion, s
circumference	s

circumstance	s
circus	es
cistern	s
citizen	s
cit y	ies
civil	ity, ly
civilian	s
civilize	d, ɇing, ɇation, s

cl

claim	ed, ing, s
clamber	ed, ing, s
clamm y	ier, iest, ily, iness
clamp	ed, ing, s
clang	ed, ing, s
clank	ed, ing, s
clap	ped, ping, per, s
clash	ed, ing, es
clasp	ed, ing, s
class	ed, ing, es, rooms
classic	al, s
clatter	ed, ing, s
claw	ed, ing, s
clay	ey, /pigeon, /pipe, s
clean	ed, ing, er, est, ly, ness, s
cleanliness	
cleanse	d, ɇing, r, s
clear	ed, ing, er, est, ly, ness, s
clench	ed, ing, es
clergy	man, men, woman, women
clerk	s
clever	er, est, ly, ness
click	ed, ing, s
client	s
cliff	side, -top, s
climate	s
climb	ed, ing, er, s

* chute
  shoot

cling	ing, film, s
clinic	al, ally, s
clink	ed, ing, er, s
clip	ped, ping, per, board, s
cloak	ed, ing, room, s
clock	ed, ing, wise, work, /tower, s
cloister	ed, ing, s
close (shut)	d, ∅ing, ∅ure, s
close (near; stuffy)	r, st, ly, ness
cloth	s
clothe	d, ∅ing, s
clothes	/basket, /horse, /line, -peg
cloud	ed, ing, less, lessly, burst, s
cloudy	ier, iest, ily, iness
clover	s
clown	ed, ing, s
club	bed, bing, house, s
cluck	ed, ing, s
clue	less, s
clump	ed, ing, s
clumsy	ier, iest, ily, iness
clung	
cluster	ed, ing, s
clutch	ed, ing, es
clutter	ed, ing, s

CO

coach	man, men, ed, ing, es
coal	man, men, /mine, /miner, /scuttle, s
coarse* (rough)	r, st, ly, ness
coast	al, ed, ing, line, guard, s
coat	ed, ing, -hanger, s
coax	ed, ing, es
cobble	d, ∅ing, r, stone, s
cobra	s
cobweb	by, s
cock	ed, ing, pit, tail, s
cockatoo	s
cockerel	s
cockle	shell, s
cockney	s
cockroach	es
cocoa	
coconut	/matting, /milk, /palm, s
cocoon	s
code	d, ∅ing, -breaker, /word, s
coffee	/bar, /bean, /cup, /pot, /table, s
coffin	s
coil	ed, ing, s
coin	age, ed, ing, s
coincide	d, ∅ing, s
coincidence	s
cold	er, est, ish, ly, ness, /storage, s
coleslaw	
collaborate	d, ∅ing, ∅ion, ∅or, s
collapse	d, ∅ing, ∅ible, s
collar	bone, /stud, s
collect	ed, ing, able, ion, or, s
college	/lecturer, /student, s
collide	d, ∅ing, s
collision	s
collie	s
colonel* (officer)	s
colonize	d, ∅ing, ∅ation, s
colony	ies
colossal	ly
colour	ed, ing, ful, less, /scheme, s
column	s
comb	ed, ing, s
combat	ed, ing, s
combination	s
combine	d, ∅ing, /harvester, s
come	∅ing, s
comedian	s

comed*y*	*ies*	complicate	*d, ∅ing, ∅ion, s*
comet	*s*	compliment	*ed, ing, ary, s*
comfort	*able, ably, ed, ing, s*	compose	*d, ∅ing, r, s*
comic	*al, /book, s*	composition	*s*
command	*ed, ing, er, ment, s*	comprehensive school	*s*
commando	*s*	computer	*/game, /program, s*
commemorate	*d, ∅ing, ∅ation, s*	comrade	*ship, s*
commence	*d, ∅ing, ment, s*	conceal	*ed, ing, ment, s*
comment	*ed, ing, ator, s*	conceit	*ed, edly*
commentar*y*	*ies*	concentrate	*d, ∅ing, ∅ion, s*
commerce		concern	*ed, ing, s*
commercial	*s*	concert	*s*
commission	*ed, ing, aire, er, s*	concession	*s*
commit	*ted, ting, ment, s*	conclude	*d, ∅ing, s*
committee	*s*	conclusion	*s*
common	*er, est, ly, place, /room, s*	concrete	*d, ∅ing, s*
commotion	*s*	condemn	*ed, ing, ation, s*
communicate	*d, ∅ing, ∅ion, s*	condense	*d, ∅ing, ∅ation, s*
communion		condition	*ed, ing, er, s*
communit*y*	*ies*	conduct	*ed, ing, or, s*
compact	*/disc, s*	conductress	*es*
companion	*ship, s*	conference	*s*
compan*y*	*ies*	confess	*ed, ing, es*
comparative	*ly, s*	confession	*s*
compare	*d, ∅ing, s*	confetti	
comparison	*s*	confide	*d, ∅ing, s*
compartment	*s*	confidence	*s*
compass	*es*	confident	*ial, ially, ly*
compel	*led, ling, s*	confirm	*ed, ing, ation, s*
compensate	*d, ∅ing, ∅ion, s*	confiscate	*d, ∅ing, ∅ion, s*
compete	*d, ∅ing, s*	conflict	*ed, ing, ion, s*
competition	*s*	confront	*ed, ing, ation, s*
competitor	*s*	confuse	*d, ∅ing, ∅ion, s*
complain	*ed, ing, s*	congratulate	*d, ∅ing, ∅ion, s*
complaint	*s*	congregate	*d, ∅ing, ∅ion, s*
complete	*d, ∅ing, ∅ion, ly, s*	conjure	*d, ∅ing, s*
complexion	*s*	conjurer or conjuror	*s*

conker* (horse chestnut)	s	**convent**		s
connect	ed, ing, ion, s	**converse**	d, ⌀ing, ⌀ation, s	
conquer* (defeat)	ed, ing, or, s	**convert**	ed, ing, s	
conquest	s	**convey**	ed, ing, ance, s	
conscience	s	**convict**	ed, ing, ion, s	
conscientious	ly, ness	**convince**	d, ⌀ing, s	
conscious	ly, ness	**convoy**	ed, ing, s	
consent	ed, ing, s	**cook**	ed, ing, er, ery, book, s	
consequence	s	**cool**	ed, ing, er, est, ish, ly, ness, s	
consequent	ly	**co-operate**	d, ⌀ing, ⌀ion, s	
conserve	d, ⌀ing, ⌀ation, ⌀ative, s	**cope**	d, ⌀ing, s	
consider	ed, ing, able, ably, ate, ation, s	**copper**	s	
consist	ed, ing, ent, ently, s	**coppice** or **copse**	s	
consolation	/prize, s	**copy**	ing	
conspicuous	ly, ness	**cop** ied	ies	
constable	s	**coral**	/island, /reef, s	
constant	ly	**cord**	s	
construct	ed, ing, ion, or, s	**cordial**	s	
consult	ed, ing, ant, ation, s	**cordon**	ed, ing, s	
consume	d, ⌀ing, r, s	**corduroy**	s	
contact	ed, ing, s	**core*** (middle of apple, etc)	d, ⌀ing, s	
contain	ed, ing, er, s	**corgi**	s	
contaminate	d, ing, ⌀ion, s	**cork**	ed, ing, screw, s	
contemporar y	ies	**corn**	/cob, field, flake, s	
content	ed, ing, ment, s	**corned beef**		
contest	ed, ing, ant, s	**corner**	ed, ing, /shop, s	
continent	al, s	**cornet**	s	
continual	ly	**cornish past** y	ies	
continue	d, ⌀ing, ⌀ation, s	**coronation**	s	
continuous	ly	**corporal**	s	
contract	ed, ing, ion, or, s	**corporation**	s	
contradict	ed, ing, ion, s	**corps*** (group of cadets, etc)	**corps**	
contribute	d, ⌀ing, ⌀ion, s	**corpse**	s	
control	led, ling, ler, /tower, s	**correct**	ed, ing, ion, ly, ness, s	
convalesce	d, ⌀ing, nce, nt, s	**correspond**	ed, ing, ence, ent, s	
convenience	s	**corridor**	s	
convenient	ly	**cosmetic**	s	

cosmonaut	s	crackle	d, ∉ing, s
cost	ing, s	cradle	d, ∉ing, s
costl y	ier, iest, iness	craft	sman, smen, swoman, swomen, s
costume	s	craft y	ier, iest, ily, iness
cos y	ier, iest, ily, iness, ies	cram	med, ming, mer, s
cottage	/cheese, /garden, /pie, s	cramp	ed, ing, s
cotton	/reel, wool, s	crane	d, ∉ing, /driver, s
couch	es	crank	ed, ing, s
cough	ed, ing, er, /drop, /mixture, s	crash	ed, ing, es
could		crate	d, ∉ing, ful, s
couldn't (could not)		crater	s
council	/estate, /flat, /house, s	crave	d, ∉ing, s
count	ed, ing, er, less, down, s	crawl	ed, ing, er, s
counter	ed, ing, -attack, foil, s	crayon	ed, ing, s
counterfeit	ed, ing, er, s	craze	d, ∉ing, s
countess	es	craz y	ier, iest, ily, iness
countr y	ies	creak* (noise)	ed, ing, s
count y	ies	creak y	ier, iest, ily, iness
couple	d, ∉ing, s	cream	ed, ing, er, /cake, /cheese, /tea, s
coupon	s	cream y	ier, iest, iness
courage		crease	d, ∉ing, s
courageous	ly, ness	create	d, ∉ing, s
courgette	s	creature	s
courier	s	credit	able, ed, ing, or, /card, s
course* (track; direction; of course)	s	creek* (small bay, sea-coast inlet)	s
court*	ed, ing, ier, room, ship, yard, s	creep	ing, er, s
courtes y	ies	creep y	ier, iest, ily, iness
cousin	s	cremate	d, ∉ing, s
cove	s	crematorium	s
cover	ed, ing, s	creosote	d, ∉ing, s
cow	boy, girl, hand, shed, s	crept	
coward	ice, ly, s	crescent	s
cowslip	s	crest	ed, ing, fallen, s
		crevasse* (crack in glacier)	s
cr		crevice* (crack in rock or wall)	s
crab	/apple, /meat, s	crew	ed, ing, s
crack	ed, ing, er, s	crib	bed, bing, ber, s

* course court / coarse caught
* creak crevasse / creek crevice

cricket	/ball, /bat, /ground, /team, s	cruel	ier, lest, ly, ty
cried		cruet	s
cries		cruise	d, ∉ing, r, /liner, /ship, s
crime	s	crumb	s
criminal	s	crumble	d, ∉ing, s
crimson		crumbl y	ier, iest, iness
cringe	d, ∉ing, s	crumpet	s
crinkle	d, ∉ing, s	crumple	d, ∉ing, s
crinkl y	ier, iest, iness	crunch	ed, ing, es
cripple	d, ∉ing, s	crusade	d, ∉ing, r, s
crisp	ed, ing, er, est, ly, ness, s	crush	ed, ing, es
crisp y	ier, iest, ily, iness	crust	s
critic	al, ally, ism, s	crust y	ier, iest, ily, iness
criticize	d, ∉ing, s	crutch	es
croak	ed, ing, er, s	cry	ing
croak y	ier, iest, ily, iness	cr ied	ies
crochet	ed, ing, /hook, s	crypt	s
crockery		crystal	/ball, /clear, s
crocodile	s		
crocus	es		

cu

crook	s	Cub Scout	s
crooked	ly, ness	cube	d, ∉ing, s
crop	ped, ping, per, s	cubicle	s
croquet	/ball, /hoop, /mallet, /player, s	cuckoo	/clock, s
cross	ed, ing, er, est, ly, ness, es	cucumber	s
crossroad	s	cuddle	d, ∉ing, some, s
crossword	s	cuddl y	ier, iest, iness
crouch	ed, ing, es	cue* (hint; stick used in snooker)	/ball, s
crow	ed, ing, bar, s	cuff	/link, s
crowd	ed, ing, s	cul-de-sac	s or culs-de-sac
crown	ed, ing, s	culprit	s
crucial	ly	cultivate	d, ∉ing, ∉ion, s
crucify	ing	cunning	ly
crucif ied	ies	cup	ful, s
crucifix	es	cupboard	s
crucifixion	s	curate	s
crude	r, st, ly, ness	curator	s

curb* (hold back)	*ed, ing, s*
curdle	*d, ~~e~~ing, s*
cure	*d, ~~e~~ing, s*
curio	*s*
curiosit *y*	*ies*
curious	*ly*
curl	*ed, ing, er, s*
curl *y*	*ier, iest, iness*
currant* (fruit)	*/bread, /bun, /cake, s*
current* (flow of water, air, etc)	*s*
curr *y*	*ied, ies*
curse	*d, ~~e~~ing, s*
curt	*ly, ness*
curtain	*ed, ing, s*
curtsy	*ing*
curts *ied*	*ies*
curve	*d, ~~e~~ing, s*
cushion	*/cover, s*
custard	*/powder, /pie, /tart, s*
custom	*er, s*
cut	*ting, ter, -price, -rate, -throat, s*
cute	*r, st, ness*
cutlass	*es*
cutlery	

cy

cycle	*d, ~~e~~ing, ~~e~~ist, /track, /lane, s*
cyclone	*s*
cygnet* (young swan)	*s*
cylinder	*s*
cymbal	*ist, s*
cypress	*es*

da

dab	*bed, bing, ber, s*
dabble	*d, ~~e~~ing, r, s*

dachshund	*s*
dad	*s*
dadd *y*	*ies*
daffodil	*s*
daft	*er, est, ly, ness*
dagger	*s*
dahlia	*s*
dail *y*	*ies*
daint *y*	*ier, iest, ily, iness, ies*
dair *y*	*ies*
dais *y*	*ies*
dale	*s*
Dalmatian	*s*
dam	*med, ming, s*
damage	*d, ~~e~~ing, s*
dame	*s*
damp	*ed, ing, er, est, ly, ness, s*
dampen	*ed, ing, er, s*
damson	*/tree, s*
dance	*d, ~~e~~ing, r, /band, /floor, /hall, s*
dandelion	*s*
danger	*/sign, /signal, s*
dangerous	*ly*
dangle	*d, ~~e~~ing, s*
dank	*er, est, ly, ness*
dapple	*d, ~~e~~ing, /grey, s*
dare	*d, ~~e~~ing, devil, s*
dark	*er, est, ly, ness*
darken	*ed, ing, s*
darling	*s*
darn	*ed, ing, er, s*
dart	*ed, ing, board, s*
dash	*ed, ing, es*
data	*base*
date	*d, ~~e~~ing, /stamp, /palm, s*
daub	*ed, ing, er, s*
daughter	*s*

dawdle	d, ∉ing, r, s
dawn	ed, ing, s
day	break, dream, light, time, s
daze	d, ∉ing, s
dazzle	d, ∉ing, r, s

de

dead	beat, /end, /heat, line, lock, ness
deaden	ed, ing, er, s
deadly	ier, iest, iness
deaf	/aid, er, est, ly, ness
deafen	ed, ing, s
deal	ing, er, s
dealt	
dear* (beloved; costly)	er, est, ly, ness, s
death	ly, bed, /blow, /rate, /ray, /trap, s
debate	d, ∉ing, ∉able, r, s
debris	
debt	/collector, or, s
decay	ed, ing, s
deceit	ful, fully, s
deceive	d, ∉ing, r, s
December	s
decent	ly
deception	s
decide	d, dly, ∉ing, s
decimal	/fraction, s
decipher	ed, ing, s
decision	s
deck	ed, ing, chair, s
declare	d, ∉ing, ∉ation, s
decline	d, ∉ing, s
decode	d, ∉ing, r, s
decorate	d, ∉ing, ∉ion, ∉or, s
decrease	d, ∉ing, s
deduct	ed, ing, ion, s
deed	s

deep	er, est, ly, -freeze
deepen	ed, ing, s
deer* (animal)	skin, stalker, /park, **deer**
defeat	ed, ing, s
defect	ive, s
defence	less, lessly, s
defend	ed, ing, er, s
defiant	ly
definite	ly
degree	s
delay	ed, ing, s
deliberate	ly, d, ∉ing, ∉ion, s
delicacy	ies
delicate	ly, ness
delicious	ly, ness
delight	ed, ing, s
delightful	ly, ness
deliver	ed, ing, ance, s
delivery	ies
deluge	d, ∉ing, s
demand	ed, ing, s
demolish	ed, ing, es
demon	s
demonstrate	d, ∉ing, ∉ion, ∉or, s
dense	r, st, ly, ness
dent	ed, ing, s
dentist	s
deny	ing
denied	ies
depart	ed, ing, ure, s
department	/store, s
depend	ed, ing, able, ent, s
deplore	d, ∉ing, ∉able, s
deport	ed, ing, ation, s
deposit	ed, ing, or, s
depot	s
deprive	d, ∉ing, ∉ation, s

---

depth	/charge, s	**device**	s
deputy	ies	**devil**	ish, ry, ment, s
derail	ed, ing, ment, s	**devise**	d, ⌀ing, s
derelict	s	**devote**	d, ⌀ing, s
descant	/recorder, s	**devour**	ed, ing, er, s
descend	ed, ing, ant, s	**dew*** (moisture)	y, drop, fall, s
descent	s		
describe	d, ⌀ing, s		**di**
description	s	**diagnose**	d, ⌀ing, ⌀is, s
desert (sandy place)	/island, s	**diagram**	s
desert* (run away)	ed, ing, ion, er, s	**dial**	led, ling, ler, s
deserve	d, ⌀ing, s	**dialect**	s
design	ed, ing, er, s	**dialogue**	s
desire	d, ⌀ing, ⌀able, s	**diameter**	s
desk	/drawer, top, s	**diamond**	s
desolate	d, ⌀ing, ly, ness, s	**diar**y	ies
despair	ed, ing, ingly, s	**dictate**	d, ⌀ing, ⌀ion, s
despatch use **dispatch**	ed, ing, es	**dictionar**y	ies
desperate	ly, ⌀ion	**didn't** (did not)	
despise	d, ⌀ing, s	**die*** (small spotted cube)	**dice**
despite		**die*** (lose life)	s
dessert* (pudding)	spoon, s	**died*** (lost life)	
destination	s	**dying*** (losing life)	
destroy	ed, ing, er, s	**diet**	ed, ing, ician, s
destruction		**differ**	ed, ing, ence, s
destructive	ly, ness	**different**	ly
detach	ed, ing, es	**difficult**	
detail	ed, ing, s	**difficult**y	ies
detain	ed, ing, s	**dig**	ging, ger, s
detect	ed, ing, ion, or, s	**digest**	ed, ing, ion, ive, s
detective	s	**digit**	s
detention	s	**digital**	ly, /camera, /television
deter	red, ring, s	**dignif**y	ied, ies
deteriorate	d, ⌀ing, ⌀ation, s	**dignity**	
determine	d, ⌀ing, ⌀ation, s	**dilapidated**	
detest	able, ed, ing, s	**dilute**	d, ⌀ing, ⌀ion, s
develop	ed, ing, er, ment, s	**dim**	med, ming, mer, mest, ly, ness, s

---

*	desert	*	dew die died dying
	dessert		due dye dyed dyeing

dimension	s	**disgrace**	d, ∉ing, s
dimple	d, ∉ing, s	**disgraceful**	ly, ness
dine	d, ∉ing, r, s	**disguise**	d, ∉ing, s
dining	/hall, /room, /table	**disgust**	ed, ing, s
dingh y (small boat)	ies	**dish**	ed, ing, es
ding y	ier, iest, ily, iness	**dishearten**	ed, ing, s
dinner	/service, /table, /time, s	**dishonest**	ly, y
dinosaur	s	**dislike**	able, d, ∉ing, s
dip	ped, ping, per, s	**dismal**	ly, ness
diploma	s	**dismantle**	d, ∉ing, s
direct	ed, ing, ly, ness, ive, or, s	**dismay**	ed, ing, s
direction	-finder, s	**dismiss**	ed, ing, es
director y	ies	**disobedience**	
dirt	ied, ier, iest, ily, iness, ies	**disobedient**	ly
dirty	ing	**disobey**	ed, ing, s
disable	d, ∉ing, ment, s	**disorder**	ly, s
disadvantage	d, ous, s	**dispatch**	ed, ing, es
disagree	able, d, ing, ment, s	**dispensar** y	ies
disappear	ed, ing, ance, s	**dispense**	d, ∉ing, r, s
disappoint	ed, ing, ment, s	**display**	ed, ing, s
disarm	ed, ing, ament, s	**displease**	d, ∉ing, s
disarrange	d, ∉ing, ment, s	**dispute**	d, ∉ing, s
disaster	s	**disqualify**	ing
disastrous	ly	**disqualif** ied	ies, ication
disc or **disk**	s	**dissatisfy**	ing
discharge	d, ∉ing, s	**dissatisf** ied	action, ies
disciple	s	**dissolve**	d, ∉ing, s
discipline	d, ∉ing, s	**distance**	s
disco	-dancing, s	**distant**	ly
discontent	ed, edly, ment, s	**distinct**	ion, ive, ly, ness
discourage	d, ∉ing, ment, s	**distinguish**	able, ed, ing, es
discover	ed, ing, er, s	**distract**	ed, ing, ion, s
discover y	ies	**distress**	ed, ing, es
discus* (disc for throwing)	es	**distribute**	d, ∉ing, ∉ion, s
discuss* (talk)	ed, ing, es	**district**	s
discussion	s	**disturb**	ed, ing, ance, s
disease	d, s	**ditch**	ed, ing, es

* discus
* discuss

divan	s	dot	ted, ting, s
dive	d, ǿing, r, s	double	d, ǿing, -jointed, -decker, s
divert	ed, ing, s	doubt	ed, ing, less, er, s
diversion	s	doubtful	ly, ness
divide	d, ǿing, r, s	dough* (moist flour)	nut, s, y
division	s	douse	d, ǿing, s
divorce	d, ǿing, e, s	dove	cote, s
Diwali		dowd y	ier, iest, ily, iness
dizz y	ier, iest, ily, iness	down	stairs, cast, hill, fall, pour, ward, s
		doze	d, ǿing, s

do

		dozen	s or **dozen**
docile	ǿity, ly		
dock	ed, ing, er, yard, s	## dr	
doctor	s	drab	ber, best, ly, ness
document	ation, s	draft* (a rough plan)	ed, ing, s
documentar y	ies	drag	ged, ging, net, s
dodge	d, ǿing, r, s	dragon	s
dodgem	s	dragonfl y	ies
doe* (female animal)	s	drain	age, ed, ing, pipe, s
does		drake	s
doesn't (does not)		drama	tic, tist, s
doing	s	dramatize	d, ǿing, ǿation, s
dole	d, ǿing, ful, fully, s	drank	
dollar	s	drape	d, ǿing, s
dolphin	s	drastic	ally
domestic	ally, s	draught* (flow of cold air)	y, s
domesticate	d, ǿing, ǿion, s	draughts (a board game)	
dominate	d, ǿing, ǿion, s	draw	n, ing, er, s
domino	es	drawbridge	s
donate	d, ǿing, ǿion, s	drawer	s
done		drawing	/board, /paper, /pin, /room, s
donkey	/ride, s	drawl	ed, ing, s
don't (do not)		dread	ed, ing, s
doom	ed, ing, sday, s	dreadful	ly, ness
door	bell, keeper, mat, step, way, s	dream	ed, ing, land, like, er, s
dormitor y	ies	dreamt or dreamed	
dose	d, ǿing, ǿage, s	dream y	ier, iest, ily, iness

* doe
* dough

* draft
* draught

dreary	ier, iest, ily, iness
dredge	d, ∉ing, r, s
drench	ed, ing, es
dress	ed, ing, es
dresser	s
dressing	/gown, /case, /room, /table, s
dressmaker	s
drew	
dribble	d, ∉ing, r, s
drift	ed, ing, er, s
drill	ed, ing, er, s
drink	able, ing, er, s
drip	ped, ping, s
drive	∉ing, r, way, s
driven	
drivel	led, ling, ler, s
drizzle	d, ∉ing, s
drizzl y	ier, iest, iness
dromedar y	ies
drone	d, ∉ing, s
drool	ed, ing, s
droop	ed, ing, s
drop	ped, ping, per, let, s
drought	s
drove	
drown	ed, ing, s
drowse	d, ∉ing, s
drows y	ier, iest, ily, iness
drudgery	
drug	ged, ging, /addict, store, s
drum	med, ming, mer, /major, stick, s
drunk	ard, s
drunken	ly, ness
dry	ing, ness, -cleaners
dr ied	ier, iest, ily, ies
dryer or drier (noun)	s
dryly or drily	

du

dual* (two; double)	/carriageway
duchess	es
duck	ed, ing, ling, /pond, s
due* (expected; owing)	s
duel* (a fight)	led, ling, list, s
duet	s
duffel	/bag, /coat, s
dug	out
duke	dom, s
dull	ed, ing, er, est, ish, y, ness, s
duly	
dumb	er, est, ly, ness, founded
dumm y	ies
dump	ed, ing, s
dumpling	s
dunce	s
dungarees	
dungeon	s
duplicate	d, ∉ing, ∉ion, s
durab le	ility
duration	
during	
dusk	
dusk y	ier, iest, iness
dust	ed, ing, man, men, bin, pan, er, s
dust y	ier, iest, iness
dut y	ies, iful
duvet	/cover, s

dw

dwarf	ed, ing, s or dwarves
dwell	ed, ing, er, s
dwelt or dwelled	
dwindle	d, ∉ing, s

* dual due
duel dew
jewel

dy

dye* (colour)	r, s
dyed* (coloured)	
dyeing* (colouring)	
dying* (losing life)	
dyke	s
dynamic	al, ally, s
dynamite	d, øing, s
dynamo	s

ea

each	
eager	ly, ness
eagle	t, s
ear	ache, drum, phone, plug, ring, s
earwig	s
earl	dom, s
earl y	ier, iest, iness
earn* (be paid)	ed, ing, er, s
earnt or **earned**	
earnest	ly, ness
earth	quake, worm, work, s
earthen	ware
ease	d, øing, s
eas y	ier, iest, ily, iness
easel	s
east	ern, erly, ward, wards
Easter	/egg, s
eat	able, en, ing, er, s
eavesdrop	ped, ping, per, s

ec

eccentric	s
echo	ed, ing, es
éclair	s
eclipse	d, øing, s

economic	al, ally, s
economize	d, øing, s
econom y	ies

ed

eddy	ing
edd ied	ies
edge	d, øing, ways, wise, s
edible	
edit	ed, ing, s
edition	s
editor	ial, s
educate	d, øing, øor, s
education	al, ally, alist, ist

ee

eel	s
eerie	r, st, øly, øness

ef

effect	ed, ing, s
effective	ly, ness
efficiency	
efficient	ly
effig y	ies
effort	less, lessly, s

eg

egg	cup, /shell, -timer, /white, /yolk, s

ei

Eid or **Id**	
eiderdown	s
eight* (8)	s
either	

---

*	dye	dyed	dyeing	earn	
	die	died	dying	urn	

*	eight (8)
	ate

el

elaborate	d, ∅ing, ∅ion, ly, s
elapse	d, ∅ing, s
elastic	ally, ity
elbow	ed, ing, /grease, /room, s
elder	ly, s
eldest	
elect	ed, ing, ion, or, s
electric	al, /fire, /light, s
electrician	s
electricity	
electrocute	d, ∅ing, ∅ion, s
elegant	ly
elephant	s
elevator	s
elf	in, ish, **elves**
eligible	
eliminate	d, ∅ing, ∅ion, s
Elizabethan	s
elm	/tree, s
elocution	ist
elope	d, ∅ing, ment, s
else	where

em

e-mail or email	ed, ing, s
embankment	s
embark	ed, ing, ation, s
embarrass	ed, ing, es
embarrassment	s
emblem	s
embrace	d, ∅ing, s
embroider	ed, ing, s
embroider y	ies
emerald	s
emerge	d, ∅ing, s

emergenc y	ies
emigrate	d, ∅ing, ∅ion, s
emperor	s
empire	s
employ	ed, ing, ment, ee, er, s
empress	es
empty	ing, -handed
empt ied	ier, iest, ily, iness, ies

en

enable	d, ∅ing, s
enamel	led, ling, s
encamp	ed, ing, ment, s
enchant	ed, ing, ment, s
encircle	d, ∅ing, ment, s
enclose	d, ∅ing, ∅ure, s
encore	d, ∅ing, s
encounter	ed, ing, s
encourage	d, ∅ing, ment, s
encyclopedia or encyclopaedia	s
end	ed, ing, less, lessly, s
endanger	ed, ing, s
endeavour	ed, ing, s
endure	d, ∅ing, ∅ance, s
enem y	ies
energetic	ally
energ y	ies
enforce	d, ∅ing, ment, s
engage	d, ∅ing, ment, s
engine	/driver, /room, s
engineer	ed, ing, s
engrave	d, ∅ing, r, s
engrossed	
engulf	ed, ing, s
enhance	d, ∅ing, ment, s
enjoy	able, ed, ing, ment, s
enlarge	d, ∅ing, r, ment, s

enlist	ed, ing, ment, s
enormous	ly, ness
enough	
enquire or inquire	d, ∉ing, r, s
enquir y or inquir y	ies
enrage	d, ∉ing, s
enrol	led, ling, ment, s
entangle	d, ∉ing, ment, s
enter	ed, ing, s
enterprise	s
entertain	ed, ing, ment, er, s
enthusiasm	s
enthusiastic	ally
entire	ly, ty
entitle	d, ∉ing, ment, s
entrance	s
entr y	ies
envelop	ed, ing, ment, s
envelope	s
envious	ly
environment	al, alist, s
envy	ing
env ied	ies

ep

epidemic	s
epilepsy	
epileptic	
episode	s

eq

equal	led, ling, ly, s
equalize	d, ∉ing, r, s
equator	ial
equip	ped, ping, ment, s
equivalent	ly

er

erase	d, ∉ing, r, s
erect	ed, ing, ion, s
erode	d, ing, s
erosion	s
err	ed, ing, ant, s
errand	s
erratic	ally
error	s
erupt	ed, ing, ion, s

es

escalate	d, ∉ing, ∉ion, s
escalator	s
escapade	s
escape	d, ∉ing, r, /route, s
escort	ed, ing, s
Eskimo use Inuit	s
especially	
espionage	
esplanade	s
essay	ist, s
essence	s
essential	ly, s
establish	ed, ing, es
establishment	s
estate	/agent, s
esteem	ed, ing, s
estimate	d, ∉ing, ∉ion, s
estuar y	ies

ev

evacuate	d, ∉ing, ∉ion, s
evade	d, ∉ing, s
evaporate	d, ∉ing, s
eve	s

even	*ed, ing, ly, ness, s*	executive	*s*
evening	*s*	exempt	*ion, s*
event	*ful, less, s*	exercise	*d, ∅ing, /book, s*
eventual	*ly*	exert	*ed, ing, ion, s*
ever	*green, lasting, more*	exhaust	*ed, ing, ion, ible, ive, -pipe, s*
every	*body, one, thing, where*	exhibit	*ed, ing, ion, or, s*
evict	*ed, ing, ion, s*	exile	*d, ∅ing, s*
evidence	*s*	exist	*ed, ing, ence, ent, s*
evident	*ly*	exit	*s*
evil	*ly, ness, s*	exorcize	*d, ∅ing, s*
evolve	*d, ∅ing, s*	exotic	*ally*
evolution	*s*	expand	*ed, ing, s*
		expanse	*∅ion, s*
ex		expect	*ed, ing, ant, ation, s*
		expedition	*s*
exact	*ly, ness*	expel	*led, ling, s*
exaggerate	*d, ∅ing, ∅ion, s*	expense	*s*
examine	*d, ∅ing, ∅ation, r, s*	expensive	*ly, ness*
example	*s*	experience	*d, ∅ing, s*
exasperate	*d, ∅ing, ∅ion, s*	experiment	*ed, ing, al, ally, s*
excavate	*d, ∅ing, ∅ion, s*	expert	*ise, ly, s*
exceed	*ed, ing, ingly, s*	expire	*d, ∅ing, s*
excel	*led, ling, s*	explain	*ed, ing, s*
excellent	*ly*	explanation	*s*
except* (leaving out)	*ed, ing, s*	explode	*d, ∅ing, s*
exception	*al, ally, s*	exploit	*s*
excerpt	*s*	explore	*d, ∅ing, ∅ation, r, s*
excess	*ive, ively, es*	explosion	*s*
exchange	*d, ∅ing, able, s*	explosive	*s*
excite	*d, dly, ∅ing, ∅able, ment, s*	export	*ed, ing, er, s*
exclaim	*ed, ing, s*	expose	*d, ∅ing, ∅ure, s*
exclamation	*s*	express	*ed, ing, es*
exclude	*d, ∅ing, s*	expression	*s*
exclusion	*s*	expulsion	*s*
exclusive	*ly, ness*	exquisite	*ly, ness*
excursion	*s*	extend	*ed, ing, s*
excuse	*d, ∅ing, ∅able, s*	extension	*s*
execute	*d, ∅ing, ∅ion, s*		

extensive	*ly, ness*
extent	
exterior	*s*
exterminate	*d, ⌀ing, ⌀ion, ⌀or, s*
extinct	*ion*
extinguish	*ed, ing, es*
extra	*s*
extract	*ed, ing, ion, s*
extraordinary	*ily, iness*
extravagance	*s*
extravagant	*ly*
extreme	*ly, s*
extricate	*d, ⌀ing, s*

ey

eye	*d, ball, bath, brow, lid, sight, sore, s*
eyeing or **eying**	
eyelash	*es*

fa

fable	*s*
fabulous	*ly, ness*
face	*d, ⌀ing, /cloth, /flannel, s*
fact	*s*
factory	*ies*
fade	*d, ⌀ing, s*
faggot	*s*
fail	*ed, ing, ure, s*
faint	*er, est, ish, ly, ness, ed, ing, s*
fair*	*er, est, ish, ly, ness, ground, s*
fairy	*ies*
faith	*s*
faithful	*ly, ness*
fake	*d, ⌀ing, r, s*
falcon	*er, s*
fall	*en, ing, s*

false	*hood, ly, ness*
falter	*ed, ing, s*
fame	*d*
familiar	*ity, ly*
family	*ies*
famine	*s*
famish	*ed, ing, es*
famous	*ly*
fan	*ned, ning, /belt, fare, light, tail, s*
fancy	*ing*
fancied	*ier, iest, ies, iful*
fantastic	*ally*
far	*ther*, thest, away, -off, -fetched*
fare* (price of journey; food)	*s*
farewell	*s*
farm	*ed, ing, er, house, yard, s*
fascinate	*d, ⌀ing, ⌀ion, s*
fashion	*able, ably, ed, ing, s*
fast	*er, est, ness, ed, ing, s*
fasten	*ed, ing, er, s*
fat	*ted, ter, test, ness, s*
fatten	*ed, ing, s*
fatty	*ier, iest, iness*
fatal	*ity, ly*
fate* (destiny)	*d, ful, s*
father* (male parent)	*less, ly, s*
fathom	*ed, ing, s*
fatigue	*d, ⌀ing, s*
fault	*ed, ing, less, lessly, s*
faulty	*ier, iest, iness*
favour	*able, ably, ed, ing, ite, itism, s*
fawn	*ed, ing, s*
fax	*ed, ing, es*

fe

fear	*ed, ing, some, s*
fearful	*ly, ness*

---

fearless	*ly, ness*
feast	*ed, ing, s*
feat* (difficult deed)	*s*
feather	*ed, ing, y, /bed, /duster, s*
feature	*d, ∅ing, s*
February	*ies*
fed	
fee	*/payer, s*
feeble	*r, st, ∅y, ness*
feed	*ing, er, s*
feel	*ing, er, s*
feet* (plural of foot)	
feign	*ed, ing, s*
fell	*ed, ing, s*
fellow	*ship, s*
felt	
female	*s*
feminine	*∅ity*
fence	*d, ∅ing, r, s*
fend	*ed, ing, er, s*
ferment	*ed, ing, s*
fern	*s*
ferocious	*ly*
ferocity	
ferret	*ed, ing, er, s*
ferry	*/boat, ing, man, men*
ferried	*ies*
fertile	*∅ity*
fertilize	*d, ∅ing, ∅ation, r, s*
fester	*ed, ing, s*
festival	*s*
festive	*ly*
festivity	*ies*
fetch	*ed, ing, es*
fête* or **fete** (festival)	*d, ∅ing, s*
feud	*s*
feudal	*ism*

fever	*ish, ishly, s*
few	*er, est*

fi

fiancé* (male)	*s*
fiancée* (female)	*s*
fiasco	*s*
fibre	*glass, s*
fiction	*al*
fictitious	*ly, ness*
fiddle	*d, ∅ing, r, stick, s*
fidget	*ed, ing, y, s*
field	*ed, ing, sman, smen, er, work, s*
fiend	*ish, s*
fierce	*r, st, ly, ness*
fiery	*ier, iest, ily, iness*
fight	*ing, er, s*
figure	*d, ∅ing, s*
file	*d, ∅ing, s*
fill	*ed, ing, er, s*
fillet	*ed, ing, s*
film	*ed, ing, /set, /star, /studio, s*
filter	*ed, ing, -paper, s*
filth	
filthy	*ier, iest, ily, iness*
final	*ly, ist, s*
find* (found)	*ing, er, s*
fine	*d*, ∅ing, s*
fine	*r, st, ly, ness*
finger	*ed, ing, mark, nail, print, tip, s*
finicky	
finish	*ed, ing, es*
fiord use **fjord**	*s*
fir*	*/cone, /tree, s*
fire	*d, ∅ing, fighter, place, side, work, s*
fire	*man, men, woman, women*
fire	*/alarm, /brigade, /engine, /escape, s*

---

fire	/drill, /extinguisher, /station, s
firm	er, est, ly, ness, s
first	ly, /aid, -class, /floor, -hand, -rate, s
fish	ed, ing, y, es or **fish**
fisher	man, men, woman, women, s
fishing	/boat, /line, /net, /rod, /tackle
fishmonger	s
fist	/fight, s
fit	ted, ting, ter, test, ful, ly, ness, ment, s
fix	ed, ing, es
fixture	s
fizz	ed, ing, es
fizz y	ier, iest, ily, iness
fizzle	d, ∅ing, s

fl

flag	ged, ging, /day, pole, ship, staff, s
flagon	s
flake	d, ∅ing, s
flame	d, ∅ing, -thrower, s
flamingo	s
flan	s
flank	ed, ing, s
flannel	s
flap	ped, ping, per, jack, s
flare	d, ∅ing, s
flash	ed, ing, es
flash y	ier, iest, ily, iness
flask	s
flat	ter, test, ly, ness, let, s
flatten	ed, ing, s
flatter	ed, ing, y, er, s
flaunt	ed, ing, s
flavour	ed, ing, less, s
flaw	ed, less, s
flea* (insect)	/bite, -bitten, s
fleck	ed, ing, s

fled	
fledgling or **fledgeling**	s
flee* (run away)	ing, s
fleece	d, ∅ing, s
fleec y	ier, iest, iness
fleet	ing, s
flesh	-coloured, /wound
flew* (fly)	
flex	ible, ibility, ed, ing, es
flick	ed, ing, s
flicker	ed, ing, s
flier or **flyer**	s
flight	/deck, /recorder, -test, s
flims y	ier, iest, ily, iness
flinch	ed, ing, es
fling	ing, s
flint	lock, stone, s
flip	ped, ping, per, s
flirt	ed, ing, ation, s
flit	ted, ting, s
float	ed, ing, er, s
flock	ed, ing, s
flog	ged, ging, s
flood	ed, ing, gate, lit, lighting, light, s
floor	ed, ing, board, cloth, /show, s
flop	ped, ping, s
flopp y	ier, iest, ily, iness
floral	ly
florist	s
flounder	ed, ing, s
flour* (ground wheat)	ed, ing, y, s
flourish	ed, ing, es
flow	ed, ing, s
flower*	ed, ing, y, /bed, pot, /show, s
flown	
flu* (influenza)	
fluctuate	d, ∅ing, ∅ion, s

---

flue* (chimney-pipe)	/pipe, s
fluency	
fluent	ly
fluff	ed, ing, s
fluff y	ier, iest, ily, iness
fluid	s
fluke	d, ∅ing, s
flung	
flurr y	ies
flush	ed, ing, es
fluster	ed, ing, s
flute	-player, s
flutter	ed, ing, s
fl y	ies
flyer or **flier**	s
flying	/fish, /officer, /saucer, /squad

fo

foal	ed, ing, s
foam	ed, ing, /rubber, s
focus	ed, ing, es
foe	s
fog	ged, ging, horn, -lamp, /signal, s
fogg y	ier, iest, ily, iness
foil	ed, ing, s
fold	ed, ing, er, s
foliage	
folk	/dance, lore, /song, /tale, s or **folk**
follow	ed, ing, er, s
foll y	ies
fond	er, est, ly, ness
fondle	d, ∅ing, s
food	stuff, store, s
fool	ed, ing, hardy, s
foolish	ly, ness
foot	ing, hold, path, sore, work, **feet**
football	er, /player, /team, s

footprint	s
footstep	s
for*	
forbade	
forbid	den, ding, s
force	d, ∅ing, s
ford	ed, ing, s
fore* (front)	arm, ground, most, man, men
forecast	ing, er, s
forecourt	s
forehead	s
foreign	
foreigner	s
foresee	able, ing, n, s
foresight	
forest	ry, er, s
foretell	ing, er, s
foretold	
forever	more
forfeit	ed, ing, ure, s
forgave	
forge	d, ∅ing, r, s
forger y	ies
forget	ting, -me-not, s
forgetful	ly, ness
forgot	ten
forgive	n, ∅ing, ness, s
fork	ed, ing, s
forlorn	ly, ness
form	ed, ing, ation, s
former	ly
formidable	
formula	e or s
fort* (castle)	s
forth* (forward)	coming
fortification	s
fortify	ing

---

* flue
  flew
  flu

* for   fort   forth
  fore   fought   fourth (4th)
  four (4)

fortified	ies
fortnight	ly
fortress	es
fortunate	ly
fortune	-teller, s
forward	ed, ing, ly, ness, s
fossil	ize, ized, s
fought* (fight)	
foul* (dirty)	ed, ing, er, est, ly, ness, s
found	ed, ing, er
foundation	/stone, s
foundry	ies
fountain	/pen, s
fowl* (bird)	s or **fowl**
fox	es, /cub, hole, hounds, hunting
foxglove	s
foyer	s

fr

fraction	s
fracture	d, ∅ing, s
fragile	∅ity
fragment	s
fragrance	s
fragrant	ly
frail	er, est, ly, ty, ness
frame	d, ∅ing, r, work, s
frank	er, est, ly, ness
frankincense	
frantic	ally
fraud	ulent, ster, s
fray	ed, ing, s
freak	ish, s
freckle	d, ∅ing, -faced, s
free	d, ing, r, st, ly, dom, style, way, s
freeze* (turn into ice)	∅ing, r, s
freight	er, s

frequent	ly, ed, ing, s
fresh	er, est, ly, ness
freshen	ed, ing, er, s
fret	ted, ting, ful, fully, s
fret	work, saw, s
friar	s
Friday	s
fridge (refrigerator)	s
fried	
friend	ship, s
friendly	ier, iest, iness
frieze* (wall decoration)	s
frigate	s
fright	s
frighten	ed, ing, s
frightful	ly, ness
frill	ed, ing, y, s
fringe	d, ∅ing, s
frisk	ed, ing, s
frisky	ier, iest, ily, iness
fritter	ed, ing, s
frivolous	ly, ness
frizz	ed, ing, es
frizzy	ier, iest, ily, iness
frock	s
frog	spawn, s
frolic	ked, king, some, s
from	
front	/door, /garden, /room, s
frontier	s
frost	ed, ing, bite, -bitten, s
frosty	ier, iest, ily, iness
froth	ed, ing, y, s
frown	ed, ing, s
froze	n
frugal	ity, ly
fruit	/cake, /juice, /tree, s

---

frustrate	d, ∅ing, ∅ion, s
fry	er, ing
fr ied	ies

fu

fudge	
fuel	led, ling, s
fugitive	s
fulfil	led, ling, ment, s
full	er, est, y, ness
fumble	d, ∅ing, r, s
fume	d, ∅ing, s
fun	fair
funn y	ier, iest, ily, iness
function	ed, ing, s
fund	-raising, -raiser, s
funeral	s
fungus	es or fungi
funnel	led, ling, s
fur* (animal's coat)	s
furr y	ier, iest, iness
furious	ly
furl	ed, ing, s
furnace	s
furnish	ed, ing, ings, es
furniture	
furrow	ed, ing, s
further	ed, ing, more, most, s
furthest	
furtive	ly, ness
fur y	ies
furze	
fuse	d, ∅ing, s
fuselage	s
fuss	ed, ing, es
fuss y	ier, iest, ily, iness
futile	ly

future	s
fuzz y	ier, iest, ily, iness

ga

gabble	d, ∅ing, r, s
gadget	s
gag	ged, ging, s
gaiety	
gaily	
gain	ed, ing, s
gait* (way of walking)	s
gala	s
galactic	
galax y	ies
gale	s
gallant	ly, s
galleon	s
galler y	ies
galley	/slave, s
gallon	s
gallop	ed, ing, s
gallows	
gamble* (bet)	d, ∅ing, r, s
gambol* (leap; frisk)	led, ling, s
game	ly, ness, keeper, s
gander	s
gang	ed, ing, ster, s
gangway	s
gaol use jail	ed, ing, er, s
gape	d, ∅ing, r, s
garage	d, ∅ing, s
garbage	
garden	ed, ing, er, /centre, /shed, s
gargle	d, ∅ing, s
garland	ed, ing, s
garlic	
garment	s

---

*	fur
	fir

*	gait	gamble
	gate	gambol

garrison	*ed, ing, s*	geometr*y*	*ic, ical, ically*	
garter	*s*	**Georgian**	*s*	
gas	*sed, sing, es*	geranium	*s*	
gash	*ed, ing, es*	gerbil	*s*	
gasp	*ed, ing, s*	germ	*s*	
gate* (door)	*keeper, post, way, s*	germinate	*d, ∉ing, ∉ion, s*	
gateau	*s* or *x*	gesticulate	*d, ∉ing, ∉ion, s*	
gather	*ed, ing, er, s*	gesture	*d, ∉ing, s*	
gaud*y*	*ier, iest, ily, iness*	get	*ting, ter, away, s*	
gauge	*d, ∉ing, s*	geyser	*s*	
gauntlet	*s*			
gauze	*s*			

gh

gave	
gay	*er, est*
gaily	
gaze	*d, ∉ing, r, s*

ghastl*y*	*ier, iest, iness*
ghetto	*s*
ghost	*s*
ghostl*y*	*ier, iest, iness*

ge

gear	*ed, ing, /lever, wheel, s*
geese	
Geiger counter	*s*
gem	*stone, s*
general	*s*
generalize	*d, ∉ing, ∉ation, s*
generally	
generate	*d, ∉ing, ∉or, s*
generation	*s*
generosity	
generous	*ly*
genie	*s* or **genii**
genius	*es*
gentle	*r, st, ness, man, men*
gently	
genuine	*ly, ness*
geograph*y*	*ical, ically*
geologist	*s*
geolog*y*	*ical, ically*

gi

giant	*s*
gidd*y*	*ier, iest, ily, iness*
gift	*ed, /shop, /token, s*
gigantic	*ally*
giggle	*d, ∉ing, r, s*
gild* (cover with gold)	*ed, ing, er, s*
gilt* (gold covering)	
ginger	*/ale, /beer, bread, /snap, s*
Gips*y* or **Gyps***y*	*ies*
giraffe	*s*
girder	*s*
girl	*ish, friend, s*
Girl Guide	*s*
give	*n, ∉ing, r, s*

gl

glacier	*s*
glad	*der, dest, ly, ness*

---

*	gate	gild	gilt
	gait	guild	guilt

gladden	*ed, ing, s*
glade	*s*
gladiator	*s*
glamorous	*ly*
glamour	
glance	*d, ∅ing, s*
glare	*d, ∅ing, s*
glass	*es*
gleam	*ed, ing, s*
glean	*ed, ing, er, s*
glee	*ful, fully*
glen	*s*
glide	*d, ∅ing, r, s*
glimmer	*ed, ing, s*
glimpse	*d, ∅ing, s*
glint	*ed, ing, s*
glisten	*ed, ing, s*
glitter	*ed, ing, s*
gloat	*ed, ing, s*
globe	*-trotter, s*
glockenspiel	*s*
gloom	
gloom *y*	*ier, iest, ily, iness*
glor *y*	*ied, ies*
glorious	*ly*
gloss *y*	*ier, iest, ily, iness*
glove	*/puppet, s*
glow	*ed, ing, -worm, s*
glue	*d, ∅ing, y, -pot, s*
glum	*mer, mest, ly, ness*

gn

gnash	*ed, ing, es*
gnat	*/bite, s*
gnaw	*n, ed, ing, er, s*
gnome	*s*

go

goal	*keeper, /kick, mouth, /post, s*
goat	*herd, skin, s*
gobble	*d, ∅ing, r, s*
goblet	*s*
goblin	*s*
god	*son, father, mother, parent, s*
godchild	*ren*
god-daughter	*s*
goddess	*es*
goes	
going	*s*
goggle	*d, ∅ing, s*
gold	*en, /coin, /dust, /mine, smith, s*
goldfish	*es* or **goldfish**
golf	*/ball, /bag, /club, /course, er, s*
gondola	*s*
gondolier	*s*
gone	
gong	*s*
good	*-hearted, -tempered, will, ness, s*
goodbye	*s*
goose	**geese**
goosebumps	
gooseberr *y*	*ies*
gore	*d, ∅ing, s*
gorge	*d, ∅ing, s*
gorgeous	*ly, ness*
gorilla* (a large ape)	*s*
gorse	*s*
gor *y*	*ier, iest*
gosling	*s*
gossip	*ed, ing, er, s*
govern	*ed, ing, or, ment, s*
governess	*es*
gown	*s*

* gorilla
  guerrilla

gr

grab	bed, bing, ber, s
grace	d, ∅ing, s
graceful	ly, ness
gracious	ly, ness
grade	d, ∅ing, s
gradient	s
gradual	ly, ness
graduate	d, ∅ing, ∅ion, s
graffiti	
grain	s
grammar	s
grand	er, est, ly, ness, stand
grand	father, pa, mother, ma, parents
grandad	s
grandchild	ren
granny	ies
grange	s
granite	
grant	ed, ing, s
Granth (Sikh holy book)	
grape	fruit, vine, s
graph	ed, ing, ic, /paper, s
grapple	d, ∅ing, s
grasp	ed, ing, s
grass	ed, ing, es
grassy	ier, iest, iness
grasshopper	s
grate* (fireplace; rub)	r*, d, ∅ing, s
grateful	ly, ness
gratitude	
grave	r, st, ly, ness
grave	digger, stone, yard, s
gravel	led, ling, ly, /path, s
gravity	ies
gravy	ies
graze	d, ∅ing, s

grease	d, ∅ing, r, paint, proof, s
greasy	ier, iest, ily, iness
great* (large)	er*, est, ly, ness
greed	
greedy	ier, iest, ily, iness
green	er, est, ly, ness, ery, ish, y, s
greengrocer	s
greenhouse	s
greet	ed, ing, s
grenade	s
grenadier	s
grew	
grey	er, est, ness, ish, -haired, hound, s
grief	-stricken, s
grieve	d, ∅ing, ∅ance, s
grievous	ly
grill* (cook)	ed, ing, er, s
grille* (grating)	s
grim	mer, mest, ly, ness
grimace	d, ∅ing, s
grime	∅y
grin	ned, ning, ner, s
grind	ing, er, stone, s
grip	ped, ping, per, s
gristle	∅y
grit	ted, ting, ty, ter, s
grizzle	d, ∅ing, ∅y, r, s
groan* (moan)	ed, ing, er, s
grocer	s
grocery	ies
groom	ed, ing, s
groove	d, ∅ing, s
grope	d, ∅ing, s
grotesque	ly, ness
grotto	es or s
ground	ed, ing, sheet, sman, smen, s
group	ed, ing, -leader, s

---

*	grate	grater
	great	greater

*	grill	groan
	grille	grown

grouse	d, ∅ing, r, s	gun	ned, ning, ner, man, men, boat, s
grove	s	gun	fire, point, powder, shot, smith, s
grovel	led, ling, ler, s	gurdwara	
grow	th, ing, er, s	gurgle	d, ∅ing, s
grown* (got bigger)		gush	ed, ing, es
grown-up	s	gust	ed, ing, s
growl	ed, ing, er, s	gust y	ier, iest, ily, iness
grub	bed, bing, ber, s	gut	ted, ting, s
grubb y	ier, iest, ily, iness	gutter	s
grudge	d, ∅ing, s	guy	s
gruelling		guzzle	d, ∅ing, r, s
gruesome	ly, ness		
gruff	er, est, ly, ness		
grumble	d, ∅ing, r, s		
grump y	ier, iest, ily, iness		
grunt	ed, ing, er, s		

gy

gymkhana	s
gymnasium	s or gymnasia
gymnast	ic, s
gymslip	s
Gyps y or Gips y	ies

gu

guarantee	d, ing, s
guard	ed, ing, sman, smen, room, s
guardian	s
guerrilla* (a fighter)	s
guess	ed*, ing, es, work
guest* (visitor)	/house, /night, /room, s
guide	d, ∅ing, /dog, /book, line, post, s
guild* (society)	hall, s
guillotine	d, ∅ing, s
guilt* (wrongdoing)	less
guilt y	ier, iest, ily, iness
guinea pig	s
guitar	ist, s
gulf	s
gull	s
gull y	ies
gulp	ed, ing, s
gum	med, ming, boil, /tree, s
gumm y	ier, iest, iness

ha

habit	s
hack	ed, ing, er, s
haddock	haddock
hadn't (had not)	
hail	ed, ing, er, stone, storm, s
hair*	dresser, dryer, pin, slide, style, s
hair y	ier, iest, iness
hake	hake
half	-price, -term, -time, way, halves
hall* (room; passage)	way, s
hallo or hello	s
Hallowe'en	s
halt	ed, ing, s
halve	d, ∅ing, s
hamburger	s

*	grown	guerrilla	guessed	guild	guilt	*	hair	hall
	groan	gorilla	guest	gild	gilt		hare	haul

hammer	ed, ing, s	**hasten**		ed, ing, s
hammock	s	**hast**y		ier, iest, ily, iness
hamper	ed, ing, s	**hat**	band, peg, pin, stand, -trick, ful, s	
hamster	s	**hatch**		ed, ing, es
hand	ed, ing, bag, work, writing, ful, s	**hatchet**		s
handcuff	ed, ing, s	**hate**		d, ∅ing, r, s
handicap	ped, ping, per, s	**hateful**		ly, ness
handicraft		**hatred**		
handiwork		**haughty**		ier, iest, ily, iness
handkerchief	s	**haul*** (pull)		age, ed, ing, ier, s
handle	d, ∅ing, r, bar, s	**haunt**		ed, ing, s
handsome	r, st, ly, ness	**have**		∅ing
handy	ier, iest, ily, iness	**haven't** (have not)		
hang	ed, ing, -gliding, -glider, s	**haversack**		s
hangar* (aeroplane shed)	s	**havoc**		
hanger* (for clothes, etc)	s	**haw**		thorn, s
Hanukkah or **Chanukah**		**hawk**		ed, ing, er, s
haphazard	ly, ness	**hay**	field, maker, making, rick, stack, s	
happen	ed, ing, s	**hazard**		ed, ing, ous, ously, s
happy	ier, iest, ily, iness	**haze**		s
harbour	ed, ing, /master, s	**haz**y		ier, iest, ily, iness
hard	er, est, ish, ly, ness, -hearted, ware	**hazel**		nut, /tree, s
harden	ed, ing, er, s			
hardship	s		**he**	
hare* (animal)	s			
hark		**head**	ed, ing, ache, long, light, line, way, s	
harm	ed, ing, s	**head**		master, teacher, s
harmful	ly, ness	**headmistress**		es
harmless	ly, ness	**headquarters**		
harness	ed, ing, es	**heal*** (cure)		ed, ing, er, s
harp	ist, s	**health**		/club, /food
harpoon	ed, ing, /gun, s	**health**y		ier, iest, ily, iness
harsh	er, est, ly, ness	**heap**		ed, ing, s
hart* (stag)	s	**hear*** (listen)		ing, s
harvest	ed, ing, er, /festival, s	**heard*** (listened)		
hasn't (has not)		**hearing aid**		s
haste		**heart*** (of body)		ache, broken, less, s
		hearten		ed, ing, s

---

* hangar	hare	hart	
hanger	hair	heart	

* haul	heal	hear	heard
hall	heel	here	herd
	he'll		

heart y	ier, iest, ily, iness
heat	ed, edly, ing, er, stroke, wave, s
heath	land, s
heathen	s
heather	s
heave	d, ∅ing, r, s
heaven	ly, ward, s
heav y	ier, iest, ily, iness
hectic	
he'd (he had; he would)	
hedge	d, ∅ing, hog, row, /sparrow, s
heed	ed, ing, ful, less, s
heel* (of foot)	ed, ing, s
heft y	ier, iest, ily, iness
heifer	s
height	s
heighten	ed, ing, s
heir* (one who inherits)	loom, s
heiress	es
held	
helicopter	/pilot, s
he'll* (he will; he shall)	
hello	s
helm	sman, smen, s
helmet	s
help	ed, ing, er, s
helpful	ly, ness
helpless	ly, ness
helter-skelter	s
hem	med, ming, line, s
her	self, s
herald	ed, ing, s
herb	al, alist, s
herd* (of cattle, etc)	ed, ing, sman, s
here* (in this place)	about(s), by, with
here's (here is)	
hermit	/crab, s

hero	es
heroic	ally, s
heroine	s
heroism	
heron	s
herring	-gull, s or **herring**
he's (he is; he has)	
hesitant	ly
hesitate	d, ∅ing, ∅ion, s
hew* (chop; cut)	n, ed, ing, er, s
hexagon	al, s

hi

hibernate	d, ∅ing, ∅ion, s
hiccup	ed, ing, s
hid	den
hide	∅ing, -and-seek, away, out, s
hideous	ly, ness
hieroglyphics	
high	er*, est, ly, chair, light, /jump, s
highland	er, s
Highness	es
highway	man, men, s
hijack	ed, ing, er, s
hike	d, ∅ing, r, s
hilarious	ly
hilarity	
hill	ock, side, top, s
hill y	ier, iest, iness
him* (he)	self
hinder	ed, ing, s
hindrance	s
Hindu	ism, s
hinge	d, ∅ing, s
hint	ed, ing, s
hippopotamus	es or **hippopotami**
hire* (rent)	d, ∅ing, -purchase, r, s

* heel   heir   herd   here
   heal   air   heard   hear
   he'll

* hew   higher   him
   hue   hire   hymn

hiss	ed, ing, es
histogram	s
historic	al, ally
history	ies
hit	ting, ter, s
hitch	ed, ing, es
hitch-hike	d, ⌀ing, r, s
hive	s

ho

hoard* (hidden store)	ed, ing, s
hoarse* (husky)	r, st, ly, ness
hobble	d, ⌀ing, s
hobby	ies
hockey	/field, /player, /stick, /team
hoe	d, ing, s
hoist	ed, ing, s
hold	ing, all, -up, er, s
hole* (hollow place)	d, ⌀ing, s
holiday	ed, ing, /camp, /maker, s
hollow	ed, ing, ly, ness, s
holly	ies
holster	s
holy* (godly)	ier, iest, ily, iness, ies
home	-grown, -made, less, work, ward, s
homely	ier, iest, iness
homesick	ness
honest	ly, y
honey	/bee, comb, dew, /pot, suckle, s
honeymoon	ed, ing, er, s
honour	able, ably, ed, ing, s
hood	ed, ing, s
hoof	beat, mark, s or **hooves**
hook	ed, ing, er, s
hooligan	ism, s
hoop	ed, ing, la, s
hooray or **hurrah** or **hurray**	s

hoot	ed, ing, er, s
hop	ped, ping, per, s
hope	d, ⌀ing, s
hopeful	ly, ness
hopeless	ly, ness
horde* (crowd)	s
horizon	tal, tally, s
horn	s
hornet	s
horoscope	s
horrible	⌀y
horrid	ly, ness
horrific	ally
horrify	ing
horrified	ies
horror	-stricken, -struck, s
horse* (animal)	back, shoe, s
horse chestnut	/tree, s
hose	d, ⌀ing, pipe, s
hospice	s
hospital	/bed, /ward, s
hospitality	
host	s
hostage	s
hostel	led, ling, ler, s
hostess	es
hostile	⌀ity
hot	ter, test, ly, ness, /dog, plate, pot
hot cross bun	s
hotel	/room, s
hound	ed, ing, s
hour* (sixty minutes)	ly, /hand, s
house	d, ⌀ing, hold, work, keeper, s
housemaster	s
housemistress	es
housewife	wives
hover	ed, ing, port, s, craft

---

however

howl — *ed, ing, er, s*

hu

huddle	*d, ∅ing, s*
hue* (colour)	*s*
hug	*ged, ging, s*
huge	*r, st, ly, ness*
hullo or **hello**	*s*
hum	*med, ming, mer, s*
human	*ity, ly, /being, s*
humble	*d, ∅ing, ∅y, r, st, ness, s*
humid	*ity*
humiliate	*d, ∅ing, ∅ion, s*
humorous	*ly*
humour	*ed, ing, s*
hump	*ed, ing, s*
hunch	*ed, ing, s*
hundred	*th, weight, s*
hung	
hunger	*ed, ing, s*
hungr *y*	*ier, iest, ily*
hunt	*ed, ing, sman, smen, er, s*
hurdle	*d, ∅ing, r, s*
hurl	*ed, ing, er, s*
hurrah or **hurray** or **hooray**	*s*
hurricane	*s*
hurry	*ing*
hurr *ied*	*iedly, ies*
hurt	*ing, s*
hurtle	*d, ∅ing, s*
husband	*s*
hush	*ed, ing, es*
husk *y*	*ier, iest, ily, iness*
hustle	*d, ∅ing, s*
hutch	*es*

hy

hyacinth	*s*
hybrid	*s*
hydraulic	*ally, s*
hydrofoil	*s*
hydrogen	
hyena	*s*
hygiene	
hygienic	*ally*
hymn* (song of praise)	*/book, /tune, s*
hypnotism	
hypnotist	*s*
hypnotize	*d, ∅ing, s*
hysteric *s*	*al, ally*

ic

ice	*d, ∅ing, berg, /cream, /cube, s*
icicle	*s*
ic *y*	*ier, iest, ily, iness*

id

Id or **Eid**	
I'd (I would; I should; I had)	
idea	*s*
ideal	*ly, ism, ist, s*
identical	*ly*
identification	
identify	*ing*
identif *ied*	*ies*
identit *y*	*ies*
idiot	*s*
idiotic	*ally*
idle* (lazy)	*d, ∅ing, r, st, ness, s*
idly	
idol* (false god)	*s*
idolize	*d, ∅ing, s*

---

ig

igloo	s
ignite	d, ∉ing, ∉ion, s
ignorance	
ignorant	ly
ignore	d, ∉ing, s
iguana	s

il

I'll* (I will; I shall)	
ill	-bred, -mannered, -treated, /health, s
illness	es
illegal	ly
illegible	
illiteracy	
illiterate	s
illuminate	d, ∉ing, ∉ion, s
illusion	ist, s
illustrate	d, ∉ing, ∉ion, ∉or, s
illustrious	

im

I'm (I am)	
image	s
imaginary	
imagine	d, ∉ing, ∉able, ∉ation, ∉ative, s
imitate	d, ∉ing, ∉ion, ∉or, s
immediate	ly, ness
immense	∉ity, ly, ness
immerse	d, ∉ing, ∉ion, s
immigrant	s
immigrate	d, ∉ing, ∉ion, s
immune	∉ity
immunize	d, ∉ing, ∉ation, s
impassable	
impatience	

impatient	ly
imperfect	ion, ly
impersonate	d, ∉ing, ∉ion, ∉or, s
impertinence	s
impertinent	ly
implement	s
implore	d, ∉ing, s
impolite	ly, ness
import	ed, ing, er, s
importance	
important	ly
impose	d, ∉ing, ∉ition, s
impossibilit y	ies
impossible	∉y
impress	ed, ing, ive, es
impression	able, s
imprison	ed, ing, ment, s
improve	d, ∉ing, ment, s
improvise	d, ∉ing, ∉ation, s
impudence	
impudent	ly
impulse	∉ive
impure	∉ity

in

inaccurate	ly
inattentive	ly, ness
incapable	
incentive	s
inch	ed, ing, es
incident	al, ally, s
incline	d, ∉ing, ∉ation, s
include	d, ∉ing, s
inclusion	s
inclusive	ly, ness
inconspicuous	ly
inconvenience	d, ∉ing, s

* I'll
  aisle
  isle

inconvenient	*ly*	initiate	*d, ∅ing, ∅ive, ∅ion, s*
incorrect	*ly, ness*	inject	*ed, ing, ion, s*
increase	*d, ∅ing, s*	injure	*d, ∅ing, s*
incredible	*∅y*	injur y	*ies*
incurable	*s*	ink	*ed, ing, /bottle, /pot, stand, well, s*
indeed		ink y	*ier, iest, iness*
indefinite	*ly, ness*	inn	*keeper, s*
independent	*ly*	inner	*most*
indicate	*d, ∅ing, ∅ion, ∅or, s*	innings	
indigestion		innocence	
indignant	*ly*	innocent	*ly, s*
indignation		inoculate	*d, ∅ing, ∅ion, s*
indistinct	*ly, ness*	inquire or enquire	*d, ∅ing, r, s*
individual	*ly, s*	inquir y or enquir y	*ies*
indoor	*s*	inquisitive	*ly, ness*
indulge	*d, ∅ing, nt, nce, s*	insane	*∅ity, ly*
industrial	*ly*	inscription	*s*
industrious	*ly*	insect	*s*
industr y	*ies*	insert	*ed, ing, ion, s*
inexpensive	*ly, ness*	inside	*s*
infant	*s*	insist	*ed, ing, ence, ent, s*
infantry	*man, /officer, /regiment*	insolence	
infect	*ed, ing, ious, ion, s*	insolent	*ly*
inferior	*ity, ly, s*	inspect	*ed, ing, ion, or, s*
inflammable		inspire	*d, ∅ing, ∅ation, s*
inflate	*d, ∅ing, ∅able, ∅ion, s*	install	*ed, ing, ation, s*
inflict	*d, ing, s*	instalment	*s*
influence	*d, ∅ing, s*	instance	*s*
influenza		instant	*aneous, ly*
inform	*ed, ing, ation, er, s*	instead	
infrequent	*ly*	instinct	*ive, ively, s*
infuriate	*d, ∅ing, s*	institute	*d, ∅ing, ∅ion, s*
ingredient	*s*	instruct	*ed, ing, ive, ion, or, s*
inhabit	*ed, ing, able, ant, s*	instrument	*al, alist, s*
inhale	*d, ∅ing, r, s*	insufficient	*ly*
inherit	*ed, ing, ance, s*	insult	*ed, ing, s*
initial	*led, ling, s*	insure	*d, ∅ing, ∅ance, s*

intact	
intelligence	
intelligent	ly
intend	ed, ing, s
intense	ly, ness
intent	ly, ness
intention	al, ally, s
interactive	ly
intercept	ed, ing, ive, ion, or, s
interest	ed, ing, s
interfere	d, ∉ing, nce, s
interior	s
intermediate	
intern	ed, ing, ment, s
international	ly
Internet	
interpret	ed, ing, ation, er, s
interrogate	d, ∉ing, ∉ion, ∉or, s
interrupt	ed, ing, ion, s
interval	s
intervene	d, ∉ing, ∉tion, s
interview	ed, ing, er, s
intimidate	d, ∉ing, ∉ion, s
intolerable	∉y
intricate	ly
intrigue	d, ∉ing, s
introduce	d, ∉ing, s
introduction	s
intrude	d, ∉ing, r, s
intrusion	s
inundate	d, ∉ing, ∉ion, s
invade	d, ∉ing, r, s
invalid	s
invasion	s
invent	ed, ing, ive, ion, or, s
invest	ed, ing, ment, or, s
investigate	d, ∉ing, ∉ion, ∉or, s

invisible	∉y
invitation	s
invite	d, ∉ing, s
involve	d, ∉ing, s
inward	ly, s

ir

iris	es
iron	ed, ing, monger, work, s
irregular	ity, ly
irrigate	d, ∉ing, ∉ion, s
irritable	∉y
irritability	
irritate	d, ∉ing, ∉ion, s

is

Islam	ic
island	er, s
isle* (island)	s
isn't (is not)	
isolate	d, ∉ing, ∉ion, s
issue	d, ∉ing, s

it

italic	s
itch	ed, ing, es
itch y	ier, iest, iness
item	s
its* (belonging to it)	
it's* (it is; it has)	
itself	

iv

I've (I have)	
ivor y	ies
iv y	ies

* isle   its
   aisle it's
   I'll

ja

jab	bed, bing, s
jabber	ed, ing, s
jack	ed, ing, pot, s
jackal	s
jackdaw	s
jacket	s
jaded	
jagged	ly, ness
jaguar	s
jail	ed, ing, er, /sentence, s
jam	med, ming, my, /pot, /jar, /tart, s
jamboree	s
jangle	d, ∉ing, s
janitor	s
Januar y	ies
jar	red, ring, ful, s
jaunt	ed, ing, s
jaunt y	ier, iest, ily, iness
javelin	/thrower, s
jaw	bone, s
jay	s
jazz	ed, ing, y, es

je

jealous	ly, y
jeans	
Jeep	s
jeer	ed, ing, s
jell y	ied, ies
jellyfish	es or jellyfish
jemm y	ies
jerk	ed, ing, s
jerk y	ier, iest, ily, iness
jerkin	s
jersey	s

jest	ed, ing, er, s
jet	ted, ting, /engine, /fighter, /plane, s
jettison	ed, ing, s
jett y	ies
Jew	ish, s
jewel*	led, ler, /case, s
jewellery	

ji

jiff y	ies
jig	ged, ging, ger, s
jigsaw puzzle	s
jilt	ed, ing, s
jingle	d, ∉ing, s
jiu-jitsu or ju-jitsu	
jive	d, ∉ing, r, s

jo

job	centre, /seeker, s
jockey	s
jocular	ity, ly
jodhpurs	
jog	ged, ging, ger, s
join	ed, ing, ery, er, s
joint	ed, ing, ly, s
joist	s
joke	d, ∉ing, r, s
jollit y	ies
joll y	ier, iest, ily, iness
jolt	ed, ing, s
jostle	d, ∉ing, s
jot	ted, ting, ter, s
journal	ism, ist, s
journey	ed, ing, s
joust	ed, ing, s
jovial	ity, ly

* jewel
   dual
   duel

joy	*ride, rider, stick, s*
joyful	*ly, ness*
joyous	*ly, ness*

ju

jubilant	*ly*
jubilation	
jubilee	*s*
Judaism	
judder	*ed, ing, s*
judge	*d, ⌀ing, ment, s*
judo	
juggernaut	*s*
juggle	*d, ⌀ing, r, s*
juice	*s*
juic y	*ier, iest, ily, iness*
Jul y	*ies*
jumble	*d, ⌀ing, /sale, s*
jumbo jet	*s*
jump	*ed, ing, er, -jet, s*
jumper	*s*
jump y	*ier, iest, ily, iness*
junction	*s*
June	*s*
jungle	*s*
junior	*s*
junk	*/food, /mail, /shop, yard, s*
junket	*s*
juror	*s*
jur y	*ies*
just	*ly, ness*
justice	
justify	*ing*
justif ied	*ies*
jut	*ted, ting, s*
juvenile	*s*

ka

kaleidoscope	*s*
kangaroo	*s*
karaoke	
karate	
kayak	*s*

ke

kebab	*s*
keel	*ed, ing, s*
keen	*er, est, ly, ness*
keep	*ing, er, sake, s*
kennel	*s*
kept	
kerb* (pavement edge)	*side, stone, s*
kernel* (nut; seed)	*s*
kestrel	*s*
ketchup	
kettle	*ful, s*
key*	*board, hole, ring, s*

kh

khaki	*s*

ki

kick	*ed, ing, -off, er, s*
kidnap	*ped, ping, per, s*
kidney	*/bean, s*
kill	*ed, ing, er, s*
kiln	*s*
kilogram(me)	*s*
kilometre	*s*
kilt	*s*
kimono	*s*
kind	*er, est, -hearted, s*
kindl y	*ier, iest, iness*

---

*	kerb	kernel	key
	curb	colonel	quay

kindness	es
kindergarten	s
kindle	d, ∉ing, s
king	dom, cup, fisher, s
kink	ed, ing, y, s
kiosk	s
kipper	s
kiss	ed, ing, es
kit	ted, ting, bag, s
kitchen	ette, /sink, s
kite	-flying, /flyer, s
kitten	s
kiwi fruit	s

kn

knack	s
knapsack	s
knave* (rogue)	s
knead* (work dough)	ed, ing, s
knee	cap, -deep, -high, -length, s
kneel	ed, ing, s
knelt or **kneeled**	
knew* (know)	
knickers	
knife	d, ∉ing, -edge, -point, **knives**
knight* (Sir)	ed, ing, ly, hood, s
knit	ted, ting, ter, s
knitting needle	s
knob	s
knobbly	ier, iest, iness
knock	ed, ing, er, out, s
knot* (tied string; sea speed)	ted, ting, s
knotty	ier, iest, iness
know* (understand)	n, ing, ingly, s
knowledge	able
knuckle	d, ∉ing, -bone, duster, s

ko

Koran	ic

la

label	led, ling, s
laboratory	ies
labour	ed, ing, er, s
lace	d, ∉ing, s
lack	ed, ing, s
lacquer	ed, ing, s
lacrosse	/player, /team
ladder	ed, ing, s
laden	
lady	ies
ladybird	s
lag	ged, ging, gard, s
lagoon	s
laid	
lain* (lie flat)	
lair* (den)	s
lake	s
lamb	ed, ing, /chop, kin, skin, swool, s
lame	d, ∉ing, r, st, ly, ness, s
lament	ed, ing, able, ation, s
lamp	light, -post, shade, /standard, s
lance	d, ∉ing, /corporal, r, s
land	ed, ing, mark, scape, slide, slip, s
landlady	ies
landlord	s
lane* (narrow path)	s
language	s
lantern	s
lap	ped, ping, top, s
lapel	s
lapse	d, ∉ing, s
larch	es

lard	*ed, ing, s*	**league**	*s*
larder	*s*	**leak*** (hole; crack)	*age, ed, ing, s*
large	*r, st, ly, ness*	**leak** *y*	*ier, iest, iness*
lark	*s*	**lean** (not fat)	*er, est, ly, ness*
larva* (insect grub)	*e*	**lean** (bend towards)	*ed, ing, s*
laser	*/beam, s*	**leant*** or **leaned**	
lash	*ed, ing, es*	**leap**	*ed, ing, frog, /year, s*
lasso	*ed, ing, es* or *s*	**leapt** or **leaped**	
last	*ed, ing, ly, s*	**learn**	*ed, ing, er, s*
latch	*ed, ing, es*	**learnt** or **learned**	
late	*r, st, ly, ness*	**least**	*ways, wise*
lathe	*s*	**leather**	*y, s*
lather	*ed, ing, s*	**leave**	*ǥing, r, s*
latitude	*s*	**lecture**	*d, ǥing, r, s*
latter	*ly*	**led*** (guided)	
laugh	*able, ed, ing, ter, s*	**ledge**	*s*
launch	*ed, ing, es*	**leek*** (vegetable)	*s*
launder	*ette, ed, ing, s*	**left**	*-handed, over, s*
laundr *y*	*ies*	**leg**	*ged, ging, less, -iron, -rest, room, s*
laurel	*s*	**legal**	*/aid, ity, ly*
lava* (volcanic rock)	*s*	**legend**	*ary, s*
lavator *y*	*ies*	**legion**	*s*
lavender	*/water*	**leisure**	*ly*
law	*ful, less, breaker, /court, s*	**lemon**	*ade, /drop, /juice, /peel, /tree, s*
lawyer	*s*	**lend**	*ing, er, s*
lawn	*-mower, -sprinkler, s*	**length**	*ways, wise, s*
lay	*ing, about, -by, out, er, s*	**lengthen**	*ed, ing, s*
laid		**length** *y*	*ier, iest, ily, iness*
layer* (coat; thickness)	*ed, ing, s*	**lenient**	*ly*
laze	*d, ǥing, s*	**lens**	*es*
laz *y*	*ier, iest, ily, iness*	**lent*** (lend)	
		leopard	*skin, s*

le

		leotard	*s*
lead* (metal)	*ed, en, s*	**less**	*er*
lead (be first)	*ing, er, s*	**lessen*** (make smaller)	*ed, ing, s*
leaf	*ed, ing, less, -stalk, y,* **leaves**	**lesson*** (thing learnt)	*s*
leaflet	*s*	**let**	*ting, s*

let's (let us)	
lethal	*ly*
letter	*ed, ing, -writer, s*
letter box	*es*
lettuce	*s*
level	*led, ling, /crossing, s*
lever	*age, ed, ing, s*

li

liable	
liar* (one who lies)	*s*
liberal	*ly, s*
liberate	*d, ¢ing, ¢ion, s*
liberty	*ies*
librarian	*s*
library	*ies*
licence* (noun)	*/fee, /holder, s*
license* (verb)	*d, ¢ing, s*
lick	*ed, ing, er, s*
licorice use **liquorice**	
lie	*d, /detector, s*
lying	
lieutenant	*/colonel, /general, s*
life	*less, like, line, long, size, time,* **lives**
life	*boat, belt, guard, /jacket, -saver*
lift	*ed, ing, er, s*
light	*er, est, ly, ness, weight, s*
light	*ed, ing, er, /bulb, house, ship, s*
lighten	*ed, ing, s*
lightning	*/conductor*
like	*able, d, ¢ing, ness, s*
likely	*ier, iest, ihood*
lilac	*/tree, s*
lily	*ies*
limb	*less, s*
lime	*/juice, light, /tree, s*
limit	*ed, ing, less, s*

limp	*ed, ing, er, est, ly, ness, s*
limpet	*s*
line	*d, ¢ing, sman, smen, s*
linen	*s*
liner	*s*
linger	*ed, ing, er, s*
link	*ed, ing, s*
lion	*s*
lioness	*es*
lip	*/balm, /gloss, salve, stick, s*
liquid	*s*
liquorice	
list	*ed, ing, s*
listen	*ed, ing, er, s*
lit or **lighted**	
literature	
litter	*ed, ing, /basket, /bin, bug, /lout, s*
little	*ness*
live	*d, ¢ing, r, s*
live (alive)	
lively	*ier, iest, ihood, iness*
liver	*ish, s*
lizard	*s*

lo

load	*ed, ing, er, s*
loaf (to idle)	*ed, ing, er, s*
loaf (bread)	**loaves**
loan* (lend)	*ed, ing, s*
loathe	*d, ¢ing, ¢some, s*
lob	*bed, bing, ber, s*
lobby	*ies*
lobster	*/pot, s*
local	*ly, s*
locality	*ies*
locate	*d, ¢ing, ¢ion, s*
loch* (a Scottish lake)	*s*

lock*	ed, ing, er, smith, s
locker	s
locomotive	s
lodge	d, ∅ing, r, s
loft	s
loft y	ier, iest, ily, iness
log	ged, ging, /book, /cabin, s
loganberr y	ies
logarithm	/table, s
loiter	ed, ing, er, s
loll	ed, ing, er, s
lollipop	s
loll y	ies
lone* (alone)	r, some
lonel y	ier, iest, iness
long	ed, ing, ingly, er, est, bow, /jump, s
longitude	s
look	ed, ing, er, out, s
looking-glass	es
loom	ed, ing, s
loop	ed, ing, hole, s
loose	r, st, ly, ness
loosen	ed, ing, s
loot* (plunder)	ed, ing, er, s
lop	ped, ping, sided, s
lord	ship, s
lorr y	ies
lose	∅ing, r, s
loss	es
lost	
lotion	s
lotto	s
loud	er, est, ish, ly, ness, speaker
lounge	d, ∅ing, r, s
lout	ish, s
love	d, ∅ing, ∅able, r, /letter, /song, s
lovel y	ier, iest, iness

low	er, est, ly, ness, s
lower	ed, ing, s
lowland	er, s
loyal	ist, ly, ty
lozenge	s

lu

lubricate	d, ∅ing, ∅ion, s
luck	less
luck y	ier, iest, ily
ludicrous	ly
ludo	
lug	ged, ging, s
luggage	/rack, /van
lukewarm	ly, ness
lull	ed, ing, s
lullab y	ies
lumbago	s
lumber	ed, ing, er, jack, /room, s
luminous	ly, ness
lump	ed, ing, s
lump y	ier, iest, ily, iness
lunatic	s
lunch	ed, ing, /box, es
luncheon	s
lung	s
lunge	d, ∅ing, s
lupin	s
lurch	ed, ing, es
lure	d, ∅ing, s
lurk	ed, ing, er, s
luscious	ly, ness
lush	er, est, ly, ness
lustre	∅ous
lust y	ier, iest, ily, iness
lute* (musical instrument)	s
luxuriant	ly

luxurious	*ly, ness*
luxury	*ies*

ly

lying	
lynch	*ed, ing, es*
lynx	*es*
lyre* (musical instrument)	*s*
lyric	*al, s*

ma

macaroni	
mace	*-bearer, s*
machine	*d, ∉ing, ∉ist, -gun, s*
machinery	
mackerel	**mackerel**
mackintosh	*es*
mad *der, dest, ly, ness, house, man, men*	
madden	*ed, ing, s*
madam (English)	*s*
madame (French)	**mesdames**
made* (make)	
magazine	*s*
maggot	*y, s*
magic	*al, ally*
magician	*s*
magistrate	*s*
magnet	*ic, ically, ism, s*
magnetize	*d, ∉ing, s*
magnificent	*ly*
magnify	*ing*
magnified	*ies*
magpie	*s*
maid* (girl)	*en, servant, s*
mail* (armour; post)	*ed, ing, s*
maim	*ed, ing, s*

main* (chief)	*ly, land, stay, s*
maintain	*ed, ing, s*
maisonette	*s*
maize* (corn)	
majesty	*ic, ically, ies*
major	*ette, /general, s*
majority	*ies*
make	*∉ing, -believe, shift, -up, r, s*
malaria	
male* (man; masculine)	*s*
mallet	*s*
mammal	*s*
mammoth	*s*
man	*ned, ning, hole, hood,* **men**
manly	*ier, iest, iness*
manage	*d, ∉ing, able, ably, ment, s*
manager	*s*
manageress	*es*
mandir	
mane* (hair)	*s*
manger	*s*
mangle	*d, ∉ing, s*
mango	*es*
maniac	
manicure	*d, ∉ing, ∉ist, s*
manipulate	*d, ∉ing, ∉ion, ∉or, s*
manner* (way; behaviour)	*ed, s*
manoeuvre	*d, ∉ing, s*
manor* (lord's land)	*/house, s*
mansion	*s*
mantelpiece	*s*
manual	*ly, s*
manufacture	*d, ∉ing, r, s*
manuscript	*s*
many	
map	*ped, ping, per, -reading, s*
marathon	*/runner, s*

---

marble	*s*
March (month)	*es*
march	*ed, ing, es*
mare* (female horse)	*s*
margarine	*s*
margin	*al, ally, s*
marigold	*s*
marine	*r, s*
marionette	*s*
mark	*ed, ing, sman, swoman, er, s*
market	*ed, ing, /day, /place, /stall, s*
marmalade	*s*
maroon	*ed, ing, s*
marquee	*s*
marriage	*s*
marry	*ing*
marr *ied*	*ies*
marrow	*s*
Mars	
marsh	*y, es*
marshal	*led, ling, s*
marshmallow	*s*
martyr	*ed, ing, dom, s*
marvel	*led, ling, s*
marvellous	*ly, ness*
marzipan	
mascot	*s*
masculine	*ǿity*
mash	*ed, ing, es*
mask	*ed, ing, s*
mason	*ry, s*
masquerade	*d, ǿing, r, s*
mass	*ed, ing, es*
massacre	*d, ǿing, s*
massage	*d, ǿing, s*
massive	*ly, ness*
mast	*ed, head, s*

master	*ed, ing, ly, y, mind, piece, s*
mat	*ted, ting, s*
matador	*s*
match	*ed, ing, sticks, wood, box, es*
mate	*d, ǿing, s*
material	*s*
mathematic	*al, ally, ian, s*
matinée	*s*
matron	*s*
matter	*ed, ing, s*
mattress	*es*
maul	*ed, ing, s*
mauve	*s*
maximum	*s* or **maxima**
may	*be*
May (month)	*s*
maypole	*s*
mayonnaise	
mayor* (head of town or city)	*s*
mayoress	*es*
maze* (puzzle)	*s*

me

meadow	*land, s*
meagre	*ly, ness*
meal	*time, s*
mean	*er, est, ly, ness, s*
meaning	*less, s*
meant	
meantime	
meanwhile	
measles	
measure	*d, ǿing, ment, s*
meat* (flesh)	*y, -axe, ball, /pie, s*
mechanic	*al, ally, s*
mechanism	*s*
medal* (badge – for bravery, etc)	*list, s*

---

medallion	*s*	messenger	*s*
meddle* (interfere)	*d, ∅ing, some, r, s*	metal	*lic, work, /detector, s*
medical	*ly, s*	meteor	*ic, ite, oid, ology, ologist, s*
medicine	*/bottle, s*	meter* (measuring device)	*s*
medieval		method	*ical, ically, s*
mediocre	*∅ity*	methylated spirit(s)	
Mediterranean		metre* (length measure)	*s*
medium	*s or media*	mew	*ed, ing, s*
meek	*er, est, ly, ness*		
meet* (come together)	*ing, s*		

mi

megaphone	*s*	miaow	*ed, ing, s*
melod y	*ious, iously, ies*	mice	
melon	*s*	microphone	*s*
melt	*ed, ing, s*	microscope	*s*
member	*ship, s*	microwave	*d, ∅ing, /oven, s*
memorial	*s*	midday	
memorize	*d, ∅ing, s*	middle	*-aged, /class, /school*
memor y	*ies*	midge	*s*
menace	*d, ∅ing, s*	midget	*s*
menagerie	*s*	midnight	
mend	*ed, ing, er, s*	midst	
mental	*ity, ly*	midway	
mention	*ed, ing, s*	might	
menu	*s*	might y	*ier, iest, ily, iness*
merchant	*s*	migraine	*s*
merciful	*ly, ness*	migrant	*s*
merciless	*ly, ness*	migrate	*d, ∅ing, ∅ion, s*
merc y	*ies*	mild	*er, est, ly, ness*
mercury		mildew	*ed, ing, s*
mere	*ly*	mile	*age, stone, s*
meringue	*s*	military	
merit	*ed, ing, s*	milk	*ed, ing, man, /bottle, /shake, s*
merr y	*ier, iest, ily, iment*	milk y	*ier, iest, iness*
mesmerize	*d, ∅ing, s*	mill	*ed, ing, er, pond, stone, s*
mess	*ed, ing, es*	millimetre	*s*
mess y	*ier, iest, ily, iness*	million	*aire, th, s*
message	*s*	mime	*d, ∅ing, s*

mimic	ked, king, s
mince	d, ⌀ing, r, meat, /pie, s
mind*	ed, ing, er, ful, less, -reader, s
mine	d*, ⌀ing, field, sweeper, s
miner* (mine worker)	s
mineral	s
mingle	d, ⌀ing, s
miniature	s
minibus	es
minimum	s or minima
minister	s
minnow	s
minor* (young person; lesser)	s
minstrel	s
mint	ed, ing, y, /sauce, s
minus	es
minute	/hand, s
minute (tiny)	st, ly, ness
miracle	s
miraculous	ly, ness
mirage	s
mirror	ed, ing, s
mirth	
misbehave	d, ⌀ing, ⌀iour, s
mischief	-maker
mischievous	ly, ness
miser	ly, s
miserable	⌀y
misery	ies
misfortune	s
mishap	s
mislay	ing, s
mislaid	
misplace	d, ⌀ing, s
miss	ed*, ing, able, es
missile	s
mission	s

missionary	ies
mist* (haze; fog)	ed, ing, s
misty	ier, iest, ily, iness
mistake	n, ⌀ing, s
mistook	
mistletoe	
mistress	es
mistrust	ed, ing, s
mitten	s
mix	ed, ing, es
mixer	s
mixture	s

mo

moan* (groan)	ed, ing, er, s
moat	ed, s
mob	bed, bing, s
mobile	/home, /phone, s
moccasin	s
mock	ed, ery, ing, s
model	led, ling, ler, s
moderate	d, ⌀ing, ly, ⌀ion, s
modern	ity, ly, ness, s
modernize	d, ⌀ing, ⌀ation, s
modest	ly, y
module	s
moist	ure, ly, ness
moisten	ed, ing, s
mole	hill, skin, s
moment	s
monarch	s
monastery	ies
Monday	s
money	/lender, /order, /spider, s
mongrel	s
monitor	s
monk	s

---

monkey	-nut, s
monotonous	ly
monotony	
monster	s
month	s
monthl y	ies
monument	s
mood	s
mood y	ier, iest, ily, iness
moon	beam, less, light, lit, s
moor	hen, land, s
moor	age, ed, ing, s
moose* (a kind of deer)	moose
mop	ped, ping, per, head, s
moral	ly, s
more	over
morning* (a.m.)	s
morsel	s
mortal	ly, s
mosaic	s
mosque	s
mosquito	es
moss	y, es
most	ly
motel	s
moth	-eaten, proof, ball, s
mother	ed, ing, less, ly, hood, s
motion	ed, ing, less, /picture, s
motor	ed, ing, bike, cycle, cyclist, s
motor	/boat, /car, /scooter, ist, way, s
motto	es or s
mould	ed, ing, er, s
mould y	ier, iest, iness
moult	ed, ing, s
mound	s
mount	ed, ing, s
mountain	ous, /bike, side, /top, s

mountaineer	ed, ing, s
mourn ing* (sorrowing)	ed, ful, fully, er, s
mouse	¢ing, ¢y, r, /hole, trap, mice
mousse* (a pudding; hair cream)	s
moustache	s
mouth	organ, ful, s
move	d, ¢ing, ¢able, ment, r, s
mow	ed, ing, er, s
mown* (cut grass, etc)	

much	
muck	ed, ing, y, -spreader, s
mud	bank, bath, guard, /pack, /pie, s
mudd y	ier, iest, ily, iness
muddle	d, ¢ing, r, s
muesli	s
muffle	d, ¢ing, r, s
mule	teer, s
multiplication	/table, s
multiply	ing
multipl ied	ier, ies
multitude	s
mumble	d, ¢ing, r, s
mumm y	ies
munch	ed, ing, es
mural	s
murder	ed, ing, er, s
murderess	es
murmur	ed, ing, er, s
muscle* (of body)	s
museum	s
mushroom	s
music	al, /lesson, /teacher, s
musician	s
musket	eer, /shot, s
Muslim	s

---

mussel* (shellfish)	s
must	
mustn't (must not)	
mustard	
must y	ier, iest, ily, iness
mutineer	s
mutiny	ing
mutin ied	ies
mutter	ed, ing, er, s
mutton	/chop
muzzle	d, ∅ing, s

my

myrrh	
myself	
myster y	ies
mysterious	ly, ness
mystify	ing
mystif ied	ies

na

nail	ed, ing, /clippers, -scissors, /file, s
naked	ly, ness
name	d, ∅ing, ly, less, /plate, sake, s
nann y	ies
napkin	/ring, s
napp y	ies
narcissus	narcissi
narrate	d, ∅ing, ∅or, s
narrow	ed, ing, er, est, ish, ly, ness, s
nasturtium	s
nast y	ier, iest, ily, iness
nation	al, ally, wide, s
nationalit y	ies
native	s

nativit y	ies
natural	ly, ness
naturalist	s
nature	/reserve, /trail, s
naught y	ier, iest, ily, iness
nautical	ly
naval	/officer, /uniform
nave* (main part of church)	s
navigate	d, ∅ing, ∅ion, ∅or, s
nav y	ies

ne

near	ed, ing, er, est, ly, ness, s
neat	er, est, ly, ness
necessar y	ily, ies
necessit y	ies
neck	lace, let, line, tie, s
nectarine	s
need* (want)	ed, ing, less, lessly, s
needn't (need not)	
needle	work, /case, s
negative	s
neglect	ed, ing, s
neglectful	ly, ness
negligent	ly
negligible	
negotiate	d, ∅ing, ∅ion, ∅or, s
neigh	ed, ing, s
neighbour	ing, ly, hood, s
neither	
nephew	s
nerve	d, ∅ing, -racking, s
nervous	ly, ness
nest	ed, ing, /egg, ful, s
nestle	d, ∅ing, s
net	ted, ting, ball, ful, work, s
nettle	s

---

* mussel
  muscle

* nave   need
  knave knead

neutral	s
never	more, theless
new* (just made)	er, est, ly, ness
news	letter, reel, -sheet, y
newsagent	s
newspaper	man, men, /boy, /girl, s
newt	s
next	

ni

nibble	d, ¢ing, r, s
nice	r, st, ly, ness
nick	ed, ing, s
nickname	d, ¢ing, s
niece	s
night*	/club, fall, /light, mare, -time, s
nightingale	s
nil	
nimble	r, st, ness, ¢y, -footed

no

no* (not any; opposite of yes)	es
noble	r, st, man, men, woman, women, s
nobody	ies
nod	ded, ding, der, s
noise	less, lessly, s
noisy	ier, iest, ily, iness
nomad	ic, s
none* (not any)	
nonsense	¢ical
noodle	s
noon	day
noose	s
normal	ly, ity
Norman	s
north	-east, -west, ern, erly, wards

nose	d, ¢ing, bag, bleed, dive, gay, s
nostril	s
not* (no)	
notable	s
notch	ed, ing, es
note	d, ¢ing, book, case, paper, let, s
nothing	
notice	d, ¢ing, able, ably, -board, s
notify	ing
notified	ication, ies
notion	s
nougat	
nought	s
nourish	ment, ed, ing, es
novel	ist, s
novelty	ies
November	s
novice	s
now	adays
nowhere	
nozzle	s

nu

nuclear	/bomb, /energy, /weapons
nude	¢ist, s
nudge	d, ¢ing, s
nugget	s
nuisance	s
numb	ed, ing, ly, ness, s
number	ed, ing, -plate, s
numeral	s
numerate	
numerical	ly
numerous	ly
nun* (religious woman)	s
nurse	d, ¢ing, maid, s
nursery	ies

*	new	night	no	none	
	knew	knight	know	nun	

*	not	
	knot	

nurture	d, ∉ing, s
nut	crackers, shell, /tree, s
nutt y	ier, iest, iness
nutmeg	s
nutrition	al, ist
nutritious	ness
nuzzle	d, ∉ing, s

ny

nylon	s
nymph	s

oa

oaf* (stupid person)	ish, s
oak	-apple, /tree, s
oar* (rowing blade)	sman, swoman, s
oas is	es
oast	-house, s
oat	meal, cake, s
oath* (promise; swear word)	s

ob

obedience	
obedient	ly
obey	ed, ing, s
object	ed, ing, or, s
objection	able, ably, s
obligation	s
oblige	d, ∉ing, s
obliterate	d, ∉ing, s
oblong	s
oboe	∉ist, s
obscure	d, ∉ing, ∉ity, ly, s
observant	ly
observator y	ies
observe	d, ∉ing, ∉ation, r, s

obsess	ed, ing, ion, ive
obsolete	
obstacle	/course, /race, s
obstinate	ly
obstruct	ed, ing, ion, s
obtain	able, ed, ing, s
obvious	ly, ness

oc

occasion	al, ally, s
occupant	s
occupation	s
occupy	ing
occup ied	ier, ies
occur	red, ring, rence, s
ocean	/liner, s
o'clock	
octagon	al, s
October	s
octopus	es

od

odd	er, est, ly, ness, ment, s
odious	ly, ness
odour	s

of

of	
off	ing, hand, chance, side, spring
offence	s
offend	ed, ing, er, s
offensive	ly, ness
offer	ed, ing, s
office	-block, -boy, -girl, -worker, s
officer	s

---

*	oaf	oar
	oath	or
		ore

official	ly, s
officious	ly
often	er, est

og

ogre	s
ogress	es

oi

oil	ed, ing, can, /rig, /stove, /well, s
oil	/heater, /painting, skin, /tanker, s
oil y	ier, iest, iness
ointment	s

ol

old	en, er, est, ish, -fashioned, -time
olive	/oil, /grove, /tree, s
Olympic Games or **Olympics**	

om

omelette	s
omen	s
ominous	ly
omission	s
omit	ted, ting, s

on

once	
oncoming	
one*	self, -sided, -way, s
onion	y, s
onlooker	s
only	
onslaught	s
onto	
onward	s

op

opal	s
opaque	ly, ness
open	ed, ing, ly, ness, er, s
opera	/glasses, /house, /singer, s
operatic	s
operate	d, ∅ing, ∅ion, s
operator	s
opinion	s
opponent	s
opportunit y	ies
oppose	d, ∅ing, s
opposite	
opposition	
oppress	ed, ing, ion, ive, es
optic	al, s
optician	s
optimist	ic, ically, s
option	al, s

or

oral	ly
orange	ade, /juice, /peel, /tree, s
orang-utan	s
orator	s
orbit	ed, ing, s
orchard	s
orchestra	l, s
orchid	s
ordeal	s
order	ed, ing, s
orderl y	iness, ies
ordinar y	ily, iness
ordinal	/number, s
ore* (metal in rock)	s
organ	/grinder, /music, ist, s

---

* one (1)
  won

* ore
  oar
  or

organism	s	outline	d, ∉ing, s
organize	d, ∉ing, ∉ation, r, s	outnumber	ed, ing, s
orient		outpatient	s
oriental	s	outpost	s
orienteering		outrage	d, ∉ing, s
origin	s	outrageous	ly, ness
original	ity, ly	outside	r, s
originate	d, ∉ing, s	outskirts	
ornament	ed, ing, al, ation, s	outward	ly, ness, s
ornithologist	s	outwit	ted, ting, s
ornithology			
orphan	ed, ing, age, s		

ov

oval	s
oven	s

os

oscillate	d, ∉ing, ∉ion, s	over	s
ostrich	es	overall	s
		overbalance	d, ∉ing, s
		overboard	

ot

		overcame	
other	s	overcome	∉ing, s
otherwise		overcoat	s
otter	s	overcrowd	ed, ing, s
		overdose	d, ∉ing, s

ou

		overflow	ed, ing, s
ought		overhaul	ed, ing, s
ounce	s	overhead	s
our* (belonging to us)	s	overhear	ing, s
ourselves		overheard	
out	come, let, look, put, right, standing	overjoyed	
outbreak	s	overlap	ped, ping, s
outburst	s	overload	ed, ing, s
outcast	s	overlook	ed, ing, s
outer	most	overpower	ed, ing, s
outfit	ted, ting, ter, s	overseas	
outhouse	s	oversleep	ing, s
outing	s	overslept	
outlaw	ed, ing, s	overtake	n, ∉ing, s

* our
   hour

overtook	
overthrow	n, ing, s
overthrew	
overtime	
overturn	ed, ing, s
overwhelm	ed, ing, s
overwork	ed, ing, s

ow

owe	d, ǿing, s
owl	et, s
own	ed, ing, er, s

ox

ox	tail, -tongue, en
oxlip	s
oxygen	

oy

oyster	/bed, catcher, /farm, /shell, s

pa

pace	d, ǿing, r, s
Pacific	
pack	ed, ing, er, s
package	d, ǿing, s
packet	ed, ing, s
pad	ded, ding, der, s
paddle	d, ǿing, r, /boat, /steamer, s
padlock	ed, ing, s
page	boy, s
pageant	s
paid	
pail* (bucket)	ful, s
pain* (suffering)	ed, ing, killer, s
painful	ly, ness

painless	ly, ness
paint	ed, ing, er, s
pair* (two)	ed, ing, s
palace	s
pale* (faint; whitish)	r, st, ly, ness, s
palette	s
palm	/tree, s
pamper	ed, ing, er, s
pamphlet	s
pan	ned, ning, ful, cake, s
panda	s
pane* (sheet of glass)	s
panel	led, ling, list, s
panic	ked, king, ky, -stricken, -struck, s
panorama	s
pansy	ies
pant	ed, ing, s
panther	s
pantomime	s
pantry	ies
paper	ed, ing, /boy, /girl, /chain, /clip, s
papier mâché	
parachute	d, ǿing, ǿist, s
parade	d, ǿing, /ground, s
paraffin	/heater, s
parallel	ed, ing, s
paralyse	d, ǿing, s
paralysis	es
paratroops	
parcel	led, ling, s
parch	ed, ing, es
parchment	s
pardon	able, ed, ing, s
pare* (cut away; peel)	d, ǿing, s
parent	age, al, s
parish	es
park	ed, ing, land, /keeper, s

---

parliament	s	pause* (hesitate)	d, ∅ing, s
parrot	s	pave	d, ∅ing, ment, s
parsley	/sauce	pavilion	s
parsnip	s	paw (animal's foot)	s*, ed, ing
parson	age, s	pawn	ed, ing, broker, shop, /ticket, s
part	ed, ing, ly, -time, s	pay	able, ing, er, ment, /day, /packet, s
participate	d, ∅ing, ∅ion, s	paid	
particular	ly, s		
partition	ed, ing, s		
partner	ed, ing, ship, s		

partridge	s	pea	nut, /pod, /shooter, s
part y	ies	peace* (quiet)	able, -offering, time
pass	ed*, ing, able, es	peaceful	ly, ness
passage	way, s	peach	es
passenger	s	peacock	s
passion	ate, ately, s	peak* (highest point)	ed, ing, s
passport	s	peal* (sound of bells)	ed, ing, s
password	s	pear* (fruit)	/drop, /tree, s
past* (time gone by)		pearl	/necklace, s
paste	d, ∅ing, s	peasant	ry, s
pastel* (crayon)	s	peat	bog, y, s
pastille* (sweet)	s	pebble	s
pastime	s	pebbl y	ier, iest, iness
pastr y	ies	peck	ed, ing, ish, er, s
pasture	d, ∅ing, land, s	peculiar	ly
past y	ies	peculiarit y	ies
pat	ted, ting, s	pedal* (foot lever)	led, ling, /cycle, s
patch	ed, ing, work, es	peddle* (to sell things at door)	d, ∅ing, s
patch y	ier, iest, ily, iness	pedestrian	s
path	way, s	pedigree	s
pathetic	ally	pedlar	s
patience		peek* (peep)	ed, ing, s
patient	ly, s	peel* (skin of fruit)	ed, ing, er, s
patio	/door, s	peep	ed, ing, er, hole, -show, s
patrol	led, ling, man, woman, s	peer* (stare)	ed, ing, s
patter	ed, ing, s	peg	ged, ging, s
pattern	ed, ing, /book, s	Pekinese	Pekinese
		pelican	s

---

* passed   pastel
  past   pastille

* pause peace peak peal pear pedal   peer
  paws   piece peek peel pair peddle pier
                            pare

pellet	s
pelt	ed, ing, s
pen	friend, /nib, s
penalize	d, ∅ing, s
penalty	ies
pence	
pencil	led, ling, /case, /sharpener, s
pendulum	s
penetrate	d, ∅ing, ∅ion, s
penguin	s
penknife	knives
pennant	s
penny	ies or pence
penniless	ly, ness
pension	ed, ing, able, er, /book, s
people	s
pepper	ed, ing, y, /pot, mint, s
perch	ed, ing, es
percussion	ist, /instrument, s
perfect	ly, ed, ing, ion, s
perform	ed, ing, ance, er, s
perfume	d, ∅ing, /bottle, s
perhaps	
peril	ous, ously, s
period	ic, ical, ically, s
periscope	s
perish	ed, ing, es
permanent	ly
permission	
permit	ted, ting, s
perplex	ed, ing, es
persevere	d, ∅ing, ∅ance, s
persist	ed, ing, ence, ent, s
person	al, ally, s
perspire	d, ∅ing, ∅ation, s
persuade	d, ∅ing, s
persuasion	

persuasive	ly, ness
pessimist	ic, ically, s
pester	ed, ing, s
pet	ted, ting, /food, /shop, s
petal	s
petrify	ied, ies
petrol	/pump, /station, /tanker, s
petticoat	s
pew	s
pewter	

ph

phantom	s
pheasant	s
philatelist	s
phone	d, ∅ing, /book, /call, /card, s
photo	/booth, fit, s
photograph	ed, ing, y, er, s
physical	/exercise, ly, s
physician	s
physics	

pi

pi* (π = 3.14159)	
pianist	s
piano	/lesson, s
piccolo	/player, s
pick	ed, ing, er, axe, pocket, s
pickle	d, ∅ing, r, s
picnic	ked, king, ker, /basket, /hamper, s
picture	d, ∅ing, /book, /frame, s
picturesque	ly, ness
pie*	crust, s
piece* (a part)	d, ∅ing, s
pier* (jetty)	s
pierce	d, ∅ing, s

*	pi	piece	pier
	pie	peace	peer

pig	*let, skin, s*
pigst *y*	*ies*
pigeon	*-hole, /loft, s*
pigm *y* or **pygm** *y*	*ies*
pigtail	*s*
pike	*man, men, staff, s*
pilchard	*s*
pile	*d, ∅ing, s*
pilgrim	*age, s*
pillar	*s*
pillar box	*es*
pillion	*/rider, /seat, s*
pillow	*case, slip, -fight, s*
pilot	*ed, ing, s*
pimple	*d, ∅ing, s*
pimpl *y*	*ier, iest, iness*
pin	*ned, ning, cushion, s*
pinafore	*s*
pincers	**pincers**
pinch	*ed, ing, es*
pine *d, ∅ing, apple, /cone, /needle, /tree, s*	
pink	*er, est, ish, y, ness, s*
pint	*s*
pioneer	*ed, ing, s*
pipe *d, ∅ing, r, -cleaner, /smoker, s*	
piranha	*s*
pirate	*s*
pistil* (part of flower)	*s*
pistol* (small gun)	*/shot, s*
pit	*ted, ting, /stop, s*
pitch	*ed, ing, /black, /dark, es*
pitchfork	*ed, ing, s*
piteous	*ly*
pity	*ing*
pit *ied*	*iful, iless, ies*
pixie	*s*
pizza	*s*

pl

placard	*s*
place* (position; put)	*d, ing, s*
plague	*d, ∅ing, s*
plaice* (fish)	**plaice**
plain*	*er, est, ly, ness, s*
plait	*ed, ing, s*
plan	*ned, ning, ner, s*
plane* (tool; to smooth)	*d, ∅ing, s*
plane* (aeroplane; tree)	*s*
planet	*s*
plank	*ed, ing, s*
plant	*ed, ing, ation, er, s*
plaster	*ed, ing, er, s*
plastic	*/bag, /cup, /surgeon, s*
Plasticine	
plate	*d, ∅ing, ful, /glass, /rack, s*
platform	*s*
platinum	
play	*ed, ing, ground, mate, time, er, s*
play	*group, /pen, thing, wright, s*
playful	*ly, ness*
plead	*ed, ing, s*
pleasant	*ly, ness*
please	*d, ∅ing, s*
pleasure	*∅able, s*
pleat	*ed, ing, s*
plentiful	*ly, ness*
plenty	
pliers	**pliers**
plod	*ded, ding, der, s*
plot	*ted, ting, ter, s*
plough	*ed, ing, man, men, s*
pluck	*ed, ing, er, s*
pluck *y*	*ier, iest, ily, iness*
plug	*ged, ging, ger, hole, s*
plum*	*/pudding, /stone, /tree, s*

---

*	pistil	place	plain	plum
	pistol	plaice	plane	plumb

plumage		pomp	ous, ously, osity
plumb*	ed, ing, /line, s	pond	/life, /snail, weed, s
plumber	s	ponder	ed, ing, s
plump	er, est, ly, ness	pontoon	/bridge, s
plunder	ed, ing, er, s	pon y	ies
plunge	d, ∉ing, r, s	poodle	s
plural	s	pool	ed, ing, s
plus	es	poor* (not rich)	er, est, ly, ness
		pop	ped, ping, per, corn, gun, s
po		pop	/group, /music, /singer, /song, s
poach	ed, ing, es	poplar	/tree, s
poacher	s	popp y	ies
pocket	ed, ing, book, /money, ful, s	popular	ity, ly
pocket knife	knives	population	s
podcast	er, ing, s	porcelain	
podg y	ier, iest, ily, iness	porch	es
poem	s	porcupine	s
poet	ic, ical, ically, s	pore* (study; tiny hole)	d, ∉ing, s
poetry		pork	/chop, /pie, er, y
pogo stick	s	porpoise	s
point	ed, ing, -blank, -duty, less, er, s	porridge	
poise	d, ∉ing, s	port	s
poison	ed, ing, ous, er, s	portable	s
poke	d, ∉ing, r, s	porter	s
polar bear	s	porthole	s
pole* (long rod)	/vault, s	portion	ed, ing, s
police	d, ∉ing, /officer, man, woman	portrait	/painter, s
police	force, station	pose	d, ∉ing, r, s
polish	ed, ing, es	position	ed, ing, s
polite	r, st, ly, ness	positive	ly, ness
political	ly	possess	ed, ing, ive, es
politician	s	possession	s
poll* (vote)	ed, ing, s	possibilit y	ies
pollen	count	possible	s
pollute	d, ∉ing, ∉ion, s	possibly	
polo	/player, /ground, /shirt, /stick	post	ed, ing, man, woman, card, mark, s
polythene		postage	/stamp

* plumb pole	* poor
plum poll	pore
	pour

postal order	s
post office	s
poster	s
postpone	d, ¢ing, ment, s
pos y	ies
pot	ted, ting, ful, luck, hole, -shot, s
potato	es
potion	s
potter	ed, ing, s
potter y	ies
pouch	es
poultice	d, ¢ing, s
poultry	
pounce	d, ¢ing, r, s
pound	ed, ing, er, s
pour* (flow out; rain)	ed, ing, er, s
pout	ed, ing, er, s
poverty	-stricken
powder	ed, ing, y, /puff, /room, s
power	ed, house, /plant, /station, s
powerful	ly, ness
powerless	ly, ness

pr

practical	ly, ity
practice* (noun)	s
practise* (verb)	d, ¢ing, s
prairie	s
praise	d, ¢ing, s
prance	d, ¢ing, s
prank	ster, s
prawn	s
pray* (ask God)	ed, ing, s
prayer	/book, /meeting, s
preach	ed, ing, es
preacher	s
precaution	ary, s

precious	ly, ness
precipice	s
precise	ly
prefect	s
prefer	red, ring, able, ably, ence, s
prehistoric	al, ally
preliminar y	ies
premises	
prepare	d, ¢ing, ¢ation, s
prescribe	d, ¢ing, s
prescription	s
presence	
present	ed, ing, ation, s
presently	
preserve	d, ¢ing, ¢ation, s
president	s
press	ed, ing, es
pressure	/cooker, /gauge, s
pretend	ed, ing, er, s
prett y	ier, iest, ily, iness
prevent	ed, ing, ion, s
previous	ly, ness
prey* (victim; thing hunted)	ed, ing, s
price	d, ¢ing, less, /list, /tag, s
prick	ed, ing, er, s
prickle	d, ¢ing, s
prickl y	ier, iest, iness
pride* (proudness)	d, ¢ing, s
pried* (looked into)	
priest	ly, hood, s
priestess	es
primary school	s
primitive	ly, ness
primrose	s
prince	ly, s
princess	es
principal* (head; chief)	ly, s

---

* pour	practice	pray
poor	practise	prey
pore		

* pride	principal	
pried	principle	

principle* (rule; truth)	s	prophec y (noun)	ies
print	ed, ing, out, er, s	prophes y (verb)	ied, ies
prison	er, /cell, /sentence, s	prophesying	
private	ly, s	prophet* (foreteller of future)	s
privilege	d, s	propose	d, ¢ing, ¢al, r, s
prize	d, ¢ing, /winner, s	proprietor	s
probabilit y	ies	prosecute	d, ¢ing, ¢or, s
probable	s	prosper	ed, ing, ous, ously, ity, s
probably		protect	ed, ing, ion, ive, or, s
problem	s	protest	ed, ing, er, s
procedure	s	Protestant	s
proceed	ed, ing, s	protrude	d, ¢ing, s
process	ed, ing, es	proud	er, est, ly
procession	s	prove	d, ¢ing, s
proclaim	ed, ing, s	proverb	s
prod	ded, ding, s	provide	d, ¢ing, r, s
produce	d, ¢ing, r, s	provision	ed, ing, s
product	ive, ion, s	provoke	ed, ¢ing, s
profession	al, ally, s	prowl	ed, ing, er, s
professor	s	prudent	ly
profit* (gain)	able, ed, ing, eer, s	prune	d, ¢ing, s
program* (for a computer)	med, ming, s	pry	ing
programme* (on television; for concert)	s	pr ied*	ies
progress	ed, ing, ion, ive, es		
prohibit	ed, ing, ion, s	pu	
project	ed, ing, ile, ion, or, s	public	/house, /school, s
promenade	d, ¢ing, r, s	publication	s
prominent	ly	publicity	
promise	d, ¢ing, s	publicize	d, ¢ing, s
promote	d, ¢ing, ¢ion, r, s	publish	ed, ing, es
prompt	ed, ing, er, est, ly, ness, s	publisher	s
pronounce	d, ¢ing, ment, s	pudding	s
proof	s	puddle	s
prop	ped, ping, s	puff	ed, ing, er, s
propel	led, ling, ler, s	puff y	ier, iest, ily, iness
proper	ly	pull	ed, ing, er, s
propert y	ies	pulley	/block, s

---

pullover	s
pulp	ed, ing, er, s
pulpit	s
pulse	d, ∮ing, s
pump	ed, ing, s
pumpkin	s
punch	ed, ing, es
punctual	ity, ly
puncture	d, ∮ing, s
punish	able, ed, ing, es
punishment	s
punt	ed, ing, er, s
pupa	e
pupil	s
puppet	ry, /show, s
puppy	ies
purchase	d, ∮ing, r, s
pure	r, st, ∮ity, ly
purple	r, st, ness, s
purpose	ly, s
purr	ed, ing, s
purse	s
pursue	d, ∮ing, r, s
pursuit	s
push	ed, ing, es
pussy	ies
put	ting, s
putt (golf)	ed, ing, er, s
putty	
puzzle	d, ∮ing, r, ment, s

py

pygmy or **pigm**y	ies
pyjamas	
pylon	s
pyramid	s
python	s

qua

quack	ed, ing, s
quadrangle	s
quadrant	s
quagmire	s
quaint	er, est, ly, ness
quake	d, ∮ing, s
Quaker	s
qualification	s
qualify	ing
qualified	ies
quality	ies
quantity	ies
quarantine	d, ∮ing, s
quarrel	led, ling, ler, some, s
quarry	ing
quarried	ies
quart (two pints)	s*
quarter	ed, ing, s
quartet	s
quartz* (rock-crystal)	
quaver	ed, ing, s
quay* (wharf)	side, s

que

queasy	ier, iest, iness
queen	s
queer	er, est, ly, ness
quell	ed, ing, s
quench	ed, ing, es
query	ing
queried	ies
quest	s
question	ed, ing, er, naire, -master, s
queue* (line of persons, etc)	d, r, s
queueing or **queuing**	

*	quarts	quay	queue
	quartz	key	cue

qui

quibble	d, ∉ing, r, s
quiche	s
quick	er, est, ly, ness
quicken	ed, ing, s
quiet	ed, ing, er, est, ly, ness, s
quieten	ed, ing, s
quill	s
quilt	ed, ing, s
quinine	
quintet	s
quire* (measure of paper)	s
quit	ted, ting, ter, s
quite	
quiver	ed, ing, s
quiz	zed, zing, zes

quo

quoit	s
quota	s
quotation	/mark, s
quote	d, ∉ing, s

ra

rabbit	ing, /hole, /skin, /warren, s
race	d, ∉ing, r, course, horse, track, s
rack	ed, ing, s
racket (tennis bat; a noise; a swindle)	s
radar	
radiant	ly
radiate	d, ∉ing, ∉ion, ∉or, s
radio	s
radish	es
radi us	i
raffle	d, ∉ing, r, /ticket, s
raft	s

rafter	s
rag	ged, ging, s
ragged	ly, ness
rage	d, ∉ing, s
raid	ed, ing, er, s
rail	ing, s
railway	/carriage, /crossing, -line, s
rain*	ed, ing, /water, bow, coat, drop, s
rain y	ier, iest, ily, iness
raise* (lift up)	d, ∉ing, s
raisin	s
rake	d, ∉ing, r, s
rally	ing
rall ied	ies
ram	med, ming, rod, s
Ramadan	
ramble	d, ∉ing, r, s
rampage	d, ∉ing, s
ramshackle	
ranch	es
rancher	s
random	ly
rang	
range	d, ∉ing, r, s
rank	ed, ing, s
ransack	ed, ing, er, s
ransom	ed, ing, s
rap* (knock)	ped, ping, s
rapid	ity, ly, s
rare	r, st, ly, ness
rascal	ly, s
rash	er, est, ly, ness
rasher	s
raspberr y	ies
rat	ted, ting, /hole, /poison, /trap, s
rate	d, ∉ing, payer, s
rather	

*	quire	
	choir	

*	rain	raise	rap
	reign	rays	wrap
	rein		

ration	*ed, ing, s*
rattle	*d, ∅ing, r, snake, s*
rave	*d, ∅ing, r, s*
raven	*s*
ravenous	*ly, ness*
ravine	*s*
raw	*er, est, ly, ness*
ray (beam of light)	*s**
razor	*/blade, /edge, /shell, s*

re

reach	*ed, ing, es*
react	*ed, ing, ion, or, s*
read* (I will read this book)	*ing, er, s*
read* (I have read this book)	
read *y*	*ier, iest, ily, iness*
real* (true)	*ly, ist, istic, ism*
realit *y*	*ies*
realize	*d, ∅ing, ∅ation, s*
really	
reap	*ed, ing, er, s*
reappear	*ed, ing, ance, s*
rear	*ed, ing, -end, guard, -light, ward, s*
rearrange	*d, ∅ing, ment, s*
reason	*ed, ing, able, ably, s*
rebel	*led, ling, lion, lious, s*
rebound	*ed, ing, s*
recall	*ed, ing, s*
recapture	*d, ∅ing, s*
recede	*d, ∅ing, s*
receipt	*s*
receive	*d, ∅ing, r, s*
recent	*ly, ness*
receptacle	*s*
reception	*ist, s*
recess	*es*
recipe	*/book, s*

recite	*d, ∅ing, ∅al, ∅ation, s*
reckless	*ly, ness*
reckon	*ed, ing, er, s*
recline	*d, ∅ing, r, s*
recognize	*d, ∅ing, ∅able, s*
recollect	*ed, ing, ion, s*
recommend	*ed, ing, ation, s*
record	*ed, ing, er, /player, s*
recover	*ed, ing, s*
recover *y*	*ies*
recreation	*/ground, s*
recruit	*ed, ing, ment, s*
rectangle	*s*
recur	*red, ring, rence, s*
red* (colour)	*der, dest, dish, dy, ness, s*
redden	*ed, ing, s*
redecorate	*d, ∅ing, s*
reduce	*d, ∅ing, s*
reduction	*s*
reed* (tall grass)	*s*
reef	*/knot, s*
reek	*ed, ing, s*
reel* (spool; dance; stagger)	*ed, ing, s*
refer	*red, ring, s*
referee	*d, ing, s*
reference	*/book, s*
reflect	*ed, ing, ion, or, s*
reform	*ed, ing, er, s*
refrain	*ed, ing, s*
refresh	*ed, ing, es*
refreshment	*s*
refrigerator	*s*
refuge	*s*
refugee	*s*
refund	*ed, ing, s*
refuse	*d, ∅ing, ∅al, s*
refuse (rubbish)	

---

*
rays	read	read	real
raise	reed	red	reel

regain	ed, ing, s	**remed** y	ies
regard	ed, ing, less, s	**remember**	ed, ing, s
regatta	s	**remembrance**	s
reggae		**remind**	ed, ing, er, s
regiment	ed, ing, al, s	**remnant**	s
region	al, s	**remote**	ly, ness
register	ed, ing, s	**remove**	d, ∉ing, ∉al, r, s
registration	s	**renew**	ed, ing, able, al, s
regret	ted, ting, table, tably, s	**rent**	ed, ing, able, al, s
regretful	ly	**repair**	ed, ing, able, er, s
regular	ity, ly	**repay**	ing, able, ment, s
regulate	d, ∉ing, ∉ion, ∉or, s	**repaid**	
rehearse	d, ∉ing, ∉al, s	**repeat**	ed, edly, ing, er, s
reign* (rule)	ed, ing, s	**repetition**	s
rein* (strap)	ed, ing, s	**replace**	d, ∉ing, able, ment, s
reindeer	reindeer	**replay**	ed, ing, s
reinforce	d, ∉ing, ment, s	**reply**	ing
reject	ed, ing, ion, s	**repl** ied	ies
rejoice	d, ∉ing, s	**report**	ed, ing, er, s
rejoin	ed, ing, s	**represent**	ed, ing, ative, s
relate	d, ∉ing, s	**reprimand**	ed, ing, s
relation	s	**reproduce**	d, ∉ing, s
relative	s	**reptile**	s
relax	ed, ing, ation, es	**reputation**	s
relay	ed, ing, /race, s	**request**	ed, ing, s
release	d, ∉ing, s	**require**	d, ∉ing, ment, s
reliab le	ility	**rescue**	d, ∉ing, r, s
relic	s	**research**	ed, ing, er, s
relief		**resemble**	d, ∉ing, ∉ance, s
relieve	d, ∉ing, s	**reserve**	d, ∉ing, ∉ation, s
religion	s	**reservoir**	s
religious	ly, ness	**reside**	d, ∉ing, nce, nt, s
reluctant	ly	**resign**	ed, ing, ation, s
rely	ing	**resist**	ed, ing, ance, s
rel ied	iable, ies	**resolution**	s
remain	ed, ing, der, s	**resort**	ed, ing, s
remark	ed, ing, able, ably, s	**respect**	ed, ing, able, ably, ful, fully, s

*   reign
    rein
    rain

responsibilit y	*ies*	**rice**	*/pudding, s*
responsible		**rich**	*er, est, ly, ness, es*
rest	*ed, ing, -cure, /home, /room, s*	**rick**	*ed, ing, s*
restful	*ly, ness*	**ricket** y	*iness*
restless	*ly, ness*	**ricochet**	*ed, ing, s*
restaurant	*s*	**rickshaw**	*s*
result	*ed, ing, s*	**ridden**	
resume	*d, ⌀ing, s*	**riddle**	*d, ⌀ing, r, s*
retire	*d, ⌀ing, ment, s*	**ride**	*⌀ing, r, s*
retrace	*d, ⌀ing, s*	**ridge**	*s*
retreat	*ed, ing, s*	**ridicule**	*d, ⌀ing, s*
retrieve	*d, ⌀ing, r, s*	**ridiculous**	*ly, ness*
return	*ed, ing, able, /ticket, s*	**rifle**	*d, ⌀ing, man, men, /range, /shot, s*
reveal	*ed, ing, s*	**rig**	*ged, ging, ger, s*
revenge	*d, ⌀ing, s*	**right*** (true; opp. left)	*ful, ly, -handed, s*
reverse	*d, ⌀ing, ⌀al, ⌀ible, s*	**rigid**	*ity, ly, ness*
review	*ed, ing, s*	**rim**	*med, ming, less, s*
revise	*d, ⌀ing, ⌀ion, s*	**rind**	*s*
revive	*d, ⌀ing, s*	**ring*** (circle)	*ed, ing, leader, master, s*
revolt	*ed, ing, s*	**ring*** (bell sound)	*ing, er, s*
revolution	*s*	**rink**	*s*
revolve	*d, ⌀ing, s*	**rinse**	*d, ⌀ing, r, s*
revolver	*s*	**riot**	*ed, ing, er, s*
reward	*ed, ing, s*	**rip**	*ped, ping, per, cord, s*
		ripe	*r, st, ly, ness*
		ripen	*ed, ing, s*

rh

		ripple	*d, ⌀ing, s*
rheumatism		**rise**	*⌀ing, r, s*
rhinoceros	*es*	**risen**	
rhododendron	*s*	**risk**	*ed, ing, s*
rhubarb		**risk** y	*ier, iest, ily, iness*
rhyme	*d, ⌀ing, s*	**rissole**	*s*
rhythm	*ic, ical, ically, s*	**rival**	*led, ling, s*
		rivalr y	*ies*

ri

		river	*/bank, /bed, boat, side, s*
rib	*bed, bing, s*	**rivet**	*ed, ing, er, s*
ribbon	*s*		

** right ring
write wring*

ro

road* (highway)	side, way, /sweeper, s
roam	ed, ing, er, s
roar	ed, ing, er, s
roast	ed, ing, er, s
rob	bed, bing, ber, s
robber y	ies
robe	d, ∉ing, s
robin	/redbreast, s
robot	s
rock	ed, ing, /cake, -climber, /pool, s
rock y	ier, iest, ily, iness
rocker y	ies
rocket	ed, ing, s
rode* (ride)	
rodeo	s
roe* (deer; fish eggs)	s
rogue	s
rôle* (actor's part)	s
roll* (turn over)	ed, ing, -call, mop, er, s
roller skate	d, ∉ing, r, s
Roman	s
romance	d, ∉ing, s
romantic	ally, s
romp	ed, ing, er, s
roof	garden, -rack, /tile, top, s
rook	s
rooker y	ies
room	ful, s
room y	ier, iest, ily, iness
root* (part of a plant)	ed, ing, s
rope	d, ∉ing, /ladder, s
rose	bud, /garden, -hip, /tree, wood, s
rosette	s
ros y	ier, iest, ily, iness
rot	ted, ting, s
rotate	d, ∉ing, ∉ion, s
rotten	ly, ness
rough	ed, ing, er, est, ly, ness, s
roughen	ed, ing, s
round	ed, ing, ish, ness, sman, smen, s
roundabout	s
rounders	
rouse	d, ∉ing, s
route* (a way)	d, ∉ing, /map, s
routine	s
rove	d, ∉ing, r, s
row (quarrel)	ed, ing, s
row* (line; use oars)	ed*, ing, er, s
rowing boat	s
rowd y	ier, iest, ily, iness, ies
royal	ist, ly, ty

ru

rub	bed, bing, s
rubber	-stamp, /tree, s
rubbish	/tip, /heap, y
rubble	
rub y	ies
rucksack	s
rudder	s
rude	r, st, ly, ness
ruffian	s
ruffle	d, ∉ing, s
rugby	/ball, /match, /player, /team
rugged	ly, ness
ruin	ed, ing, ous, s
rule	d, ∉ing, r, s
rumble	d, ∉ing, s
rummage	d, ∉ing, /sale, s
rumour	ed, ing, s
run	ning, ner, ny, way, s
rung* (ring; ladder step)	s
rural	ly, ness

---

*	road	roe	rôle	root
	rode	row	roll	route
	rowed			

*	rung
	wrung

rush	*ed, ing, es*
rust	*ed, ing, less, proof, s*
rust y	*ier, iest, ily, iness*
rustle	*d, ∉ing, r, s*
rut	*ted, ting, ty, s*
ruthless	*ly, ness*

sa

sabbath	*s*
sabotage	*d, ∉ing, s*
sack	*ed, ing, ful, /race, s*
sacred	*ly, ness*
sacrifice	*d, ∉ing, s*
sad	*der, dest, ly, ness*
sadden	*ed, ing, s*
saddle	*d, ∉ing, r, bag, s*
safari	*/park, s*
safe	*r, st, ly, ness, s*
safety	*/catch, /lamp, /net, /pin, /valve*
sag	*ged, ging, s*
said	
sail* (travel by ship)	*ed, ing, s*
sailor	*s*
saint	*ly, s*
sake	*s*
salad	*/cream, /dressing, s*
salar y	*ies*
sale* (selling)	*sman, swoman, /room, s*
salmon	*-fishing,* **salmon**
saloon	*s*
salt	*ed, ing, /water, /cellar, /spoon, s*
salt y	*ier, iest, iness*
salute	*d, ∉ing, s*
salvage	*d, ∉ing, s*
same	*ness*
sample	*d, ∉ing, r, s*
sanctuar y	*ies*

sand	*castle, /dune, paper, storm, s*
sand y	*ier, iest, iness*
sandal	*s*
sandwich	*ed, ing, es*
sang	
sank	
Santa Claus	
sap	*ped, ping, ling, s*
sapphire	*s*
sarcasm	
sarcastic	*ally*
sardine	*s*
sari	*s*
sash	*es*
satchel	*s*
satellite	*s*
satin	*s*
satisfaction	
satisfactor y	*ily*
satisfy	*ing*
satisf ied	*ies*
saturate	*d, ∉ing, s*
Saturday	*s*
sauce	*pan, /bottle, s*
saucer	*ful, s*
sauc y	*ier, iest, ily, iness*
saunter	*ed, ing, s*
sausage	*/meat, /roll, /skin, s*
savage	*d, ∉ing, ly, ry, ness, s*
save	*d, ∉ing, r, s*
saviour	*s*
saw	*ed, ing, dust, mill, s*
sawn or **sawed**	
Saxon	*s*
saxophone	*∉ist, s*
say	*ing, s*
said	

** sail
sale*

sc

scaffold	ing, s
scald	ed, ing, s
scale	d, ∉ing, s
scalp	ed, ing, s
scamper	ed, ing, s
scampi	
scan	ned, ning, ner, s
scandal	ous
scar	red, ring, s
scarce	r, st, ly, ness
scarcit y	ies
scare	d, ∉ing, r, crow, s
scar y	ier, iest, ily, iness
scarf	/ring, s or **scarves**
scarlet	s
scatter	ed, ing, -brain, s
scavenge	d, ∉ing, r, s
scene* (view; place)	s
scenery	
scent* (smell; perfume)	ed, ing, /bottle, s
scheme	d, ∉ing, r, s
scholar	ship, s
scholastic	ally
school	ed, ing, boy, girl, teacher, s
schoolmaster	s
schoolmistress	es
schooner	s
science	/fiction, s
scientific	ally
scientist	s
scissors	**scissors**
scold	ed, ing, er, s
scone	s
scoop	ed, ing, er, s
scooter	s
scorch	ed, ing, es

score	d, ∉ing, r, board, card, /sheet, s
scorn	ed, ing, er, s
scornful	ly, ness
scorpion	s
scoundrel	s
scour	ed, ing, er, s
scout	ed, ing, er, master, s
scowl	ed, ing, er, s
scragg y	ier, iest, ily, iness
scramble	d, ∉ing, r, s
scrap	ped, ping, py, book, /heap, s
scrape	d, ∉ing, r, s
scratch	ed, ing, es
scratch y	ier, iest, ily, iness
scrawl	ed, ing, er, s
scrawl y	ier, iest, iness
scream	ed, ing, er, s
screech	ed, ing, y, es
screen	ed, ing, s
screw	ed, ing, driver, s
scribble	d, ∉ing, r, s
scripture	s
scroll	s
scrub	bed, bing, ber, s
scruff y	ier, iest, ily, iness
scrutinize	d, ∉ing, r, s
scuffle	d, ∉ing, r, s
scull* (oar; to row)	ed, ing, er, s
sculler y	ies
sculptor	s
sculpture	d, ∉ing, s
scuttle	d, ∉ing, s
scythe	d, ∉ing, s

se

sea*	side, sick, shore, front, port, s
sea*	gull, /horse, /lion, /serpent, s

---

*	scene	scent	
	seen	sent	

*	scull	sea	
	skull	see	

sea*	*man, men, shell, /water, weed, s*
Sea Scout	*s*
seal	*ed, ing, er, skin, s*
sealing* (fastening)	*/wax*
seam* (join; rock vein)	*less, s*
search	*ed, ing, es*
searchlight	*s*
season	*able, al, /ticket, s*
seat	*ed, ing, er, /belt, s*
seclude	*d, ȼing, s*
second	*ly, -best, -class, -hand, -rate, s*
secondary	
secrecy	
secret	*ive, ly, /agent, /service, s*
secretary	*ies*
section	*s*
secure	*d, ȼing, ly, ness, s*
security	*ies*
see* (notice)	*ing, s*
seed	*ed, ing, y, ling, /bed, /cake, s*
seek	*ing, er, s*
seem* (appear)	*ed, ing, s*
seen* (noticed)	
see-saw	*ed, ing, s*
seethe	*d, ȼing, s*
segregate	*d, ȼing, ȼion, s*
seize	*d, ȼing, ȼure, s*
seldom	
select	*ed, ing, ion, s*
self	*-conscious, -service,* **selves**
selfish	*ly, ness*
sell* (exchange for money)	*ing, er*, s*
Sellotape	*d, ȼing, s*
semicircle	*s*
semicircular	
semi-detached	
semi-final	*ist, s*

send	*ing, er, s*
senior	*s*
sensation	*al, ally, s*
sense	*d, ȼing, less, s*
sensible	*ȼy*
sensitive	*ȼity, ly*
sent* (send)	
sentence	*d, ȼing, s*
sentiment	*al, ally, s*
sentry	*ies*
separate	*d, ȼing, ȼation, ly, s*
September	*s*
sequin	*s*
serenade	*d, ȼing, r, s*
serf* (slave)	*dom, s*
sergeant	*/major, s*
serial* (in parts – as story or film)	*s*
series	
serious	*ly, ness*
sermon	*s*
serpent	*s*
servant	*s*
serve	*d, ȼing, r, s*
service	*d, ȼing, /station, s*
serviette	*s*
session	*s*
set	*ting, ter, back, /square, s*
settee	*s*
settle	*d, ȼing, r, ment, s*
several	
severe	*r, st, ly*
severity	
sew* (stitch)	*ed, ing, er, s*
sewing machine	*s*
sewn* (fastened with stitches)	
sex	*ism, ist, y, ual, es*
sextet	*s*

---

*	sea	sealing	seam	seen	sell	seller
	see	ceiling	seem	scene	cell	cellar

*	sent	serf	serial	sew	sewn
	cent	surf	cereal	so	sown
	scent			sow	

sh

shabb y	ier, iest, ily, iness
shack	s
shade	d, ∅ing, s
shad y	ier, iest, ily, iness
shadow	ed, ing, y, s
shaft	s
shagg y	ier, iest, ily, iness
shake	n, ∅ing, r, s
shak y	ier, iest, ily, iness
shall	
shallow	er, est, ly, ness, s
shamble	d, ∅ing, s
shame	d, ∅ing, s
shameful	ly, ness
shameless	ly, ness
shampoo	ed, ing, s
shamrock	s
shand y	ies
shan't (shall not)	
shant y	ies
shape	d, ∅ing, less, s
shapel y	ier, iest, iness
share	d, ∅ing, s
shark	skin, s
sharp	er, est, ly, ness, shooter, s
sharpen	ed, ing, er, s
shatter	ed, ing, s
shave	n, d, ∅ing, r, s
shawl	s
sheaf	sheaves
shear* (cut; clip)	ed, ing, er, s
sheath	s
shed	ding, der, s
sheep	dog, /farmer, /pen, skin, sheep
sheer* (steep)	
sheet	s

sheikh	s
shelf	shelves
shell	ed, ing, s
shellfish	shellfish
she'll (she will; she shall)	
shelter	ed, ing, s
shepherd	s
shepherdess	es
sherbet	s
sheriff	s
sherr y	ies
she's (she is; she has)	
shield	ed, ing, s
shift	ed, ing, y, er, s
shimmer	ed, ing, s
shin	ned, ning, /bone, -guard, -pad, s
shine	∅ing, s
shin y	ier, iest, ily, iness
shingle	s
ship	ped, ping, load, mate, yard, s
shipwreck	ed, ing, s
shirk	ed, ing, er, s
shirt	-front, sleeve, -tail, s
shiver	ed, ing, y, s
shoal	ed, ing, s
shock	ed, ing, s
shodd y	ier, iest, ily, iness
shoe*	ing, bag, horn, lace, maker, s
shod	
shone	
shoo* (frighten away)	ed, ing, s
shook	
shoot* (fire)	ing, er, s
shop	ped, ping, per, keeper, /window, s
shore* (seashore)	s
shorn	
short	age, er, est, ly, ness, bread, s

---

shorten	*ed, ing, s*	**side**	*d, ∉ing, car, light, line, show, s*
shorthand		**sideboard**	*s*
shot	*gun, s*	**sideways**	
should		**siege**	*s*
shouldn't (should not)		**sieve**	*d, ∉ing, s*
shoulder	*ed, ing, /bag, /blade, /strap, s*	**sift**	*ed, ing, er, s*
shout	*ed, ing, er, s*	**sigh**	*ed, ing, s*
shovel	*led, ling, ler, ful, s*	**sight***	*ed, ing, less, s*
show	*n, ed, ing, case, room, s*	**sightsee**	*ing, r, s*
show	*jumper, jumping, ground, s*	**sign**	*ed, ing, board, writer, post, s*
shower	*ed, ing, -bath, s*	**signal**	*led, ling, ler, man, men, s*
shower *y*	*ier, iest, iness*	**signal box**	*es*
shrank		**signature**	*s*
shred	*ded, ding, der, s*	**signet*** (a seal)	*/ring, s*
shrewd	*er, est, ly, ness*	**significance**	
shriek	*ed, ing, er, s*	**significant**	*ly*
shrill	*ed, ing, er, est, y, ness, s*	**signify**	*ing*
shrimp	*ed, ing, er, s* or **shrimp**	**signif** *ied*	*ies*
shrine	*s*	**Sikh**	*ism, s*
shrink	*ing, able, age, s*	**silence**	*d, ∉ing, r, s*
shrivel	*led, ling, s*	**silent**	*ly*
shrub	*s*	**silhouette**	*d, ∉ing, s*
shrubber *y*	*ies*	**silk**	*en, worm, s*
shrug	*ged, ging, s*	**silk** *y*	*ier, iest, ily, iness*
shrunk	*en*	**sill** *y*	*ier, iest, ily, iness, ies*
shudder	*ed, ing, s*	**silver** *ed, ing, y, /paper, -plated, /spoon, s*
shuffle	*d, ∉ing, r, s*	**SIM card**	*s*
shun	*ned, ning, s*	**similar**	*ity, ly*
shunt	*ed, ing, er, s*	**simmer**	*ed, ing, s*
shut	*ting, s*	**simple**	*r, st, ness, ton, -minded*
shutter	*ed, ing, s*	**simplicity**	
shuttle	*d, ∉ing, cock, s*	**simply**	
shy	*er, est, ly, ness*	**simplify**	*ing*
		simplif *ied*	*ication, ies*
		simultaneous	*ly, ness*

si

sick	*er, est, ly, ness, bay, bed, room*	**sin**	*ned, ning, ner, s*
sicken	*ed, ing, s*	**since**	

---

	sight	signet
*	site	cygnet

sincere	*r, st, ly*	skipper	*ed, ing, s*
sincerity		skirmish	*ed, ing, es*
sing	*ing, er, -song, s*	skirt	*ed, ing, s*
singe	*d, ing, s*	skittle	*d, ∮ing, r, /alley, /ball, /pin, s*
single	*d, ∮ing, ∮y, -handed, s*	skulk	*ed, ing, s*
singular	*ly, s*	skull* (head bones)	*cap, s*
sinister	*ly*	skunk	*s*
sink	*ing, er, s*	sky	*ing, lark, light, rocket, scraper*
sip	*ped, ping, per, s*	sk*ied*	*ies*
siphon	*ed, ing, s*		
sister	*ly, s*		
sister *(s)*-in-law		## sl	
sit	*ting, ter, s*	slack	*ed, ing, er, est, ly, ness, s*
sitting room	*s*	slacken	*ed, ing, s*
site* (a place; website)	*d, ∮ing, s*	slain	
situated		slam	*med, ming, s*
situation	*s*	slang	*y*
size	*d, ∮ing, s*	slant	*ed, ing, wise, s*
sizzle	*d, ∮ing, s*	slap	*ped, ping, per, dash, stick, s*
		slash	*ed, ing, es*
		slate	*s*
## sk		slaughter	*ed, ing, er, -house, s*
skate	*d, ∮ing, r, board, s*	slave	*d, ∮ing, r, ry, -driver, s*
skating rink	*s*	slay* (kill)	*ing, er, s*
skein	*s*	sledge or sled	*s*
skeleton	*s*	sledgehammer	*s*
sketch	*ed, ing, es*	sleek	*ed, ing, er, est, ly, ness, s*
sketch *y*	*ier, iest, ily, iness*	sleep	*ing, er, less, walking, walker, s*
skewer	*ed, ing, s*	sleep *y*	*ier, iest, ily, iness*
ski	*ed, ing, er, /jump, /lift, /run, /slope, s*	slept	
skid	*ded, ding, s*	sleet	*ed, ing, y, s*
skilful	*ly, ness*	sleeve	*d, less, /button, s*
skill	*ed, s*	sleigh* (sledge)	*ing, -bell, s*
skim	*med, ming, mer, s*	slender	*ly, ness*
skin	*ned, ning, /diving, /diver, s*	sleuth	*s*
skinn *y*	*ier, iest, iness*	slew	
skip	*ped, ping, per, s*	slice	*d, ∮ing, r, s*
skipping rope	*s*	slick	*ed, ing, er, est, ly, ness, s*

slid

slide — ⌀ing, r, s

slight — ed, ing, er, est, ly, ness, s

slim — med, ming, mer, mest, ly, ness, s

slime

slim y — ier, iest, ily, iness

sling — ing, er, s

slink — ing, er, s

slink y — ier, iest, ily, iness

slip — ped, ping, knot, shod, way, s

slipper — s

slipper y — ier, iest, ily, iness

slit — ting, ter, s

slither — ed, ing, y, s

sloe* (wild plum) — s

slog — ged, ging, ger, s

slogan — s

slop — ped, ping, s

slopp y — ier, iest, ily, iness

slope — d, ⌀ing, s

slosh — ed, ing, es

slot — ted, ting, /machine, /meter, s

slouch — ed, ing, es

slovenl y — iness

slow* — ed, ing, er, est, ly, ness, s

slowcoach — es

slug — s

sluggish — ly, ness

sluice — d, ⌀ing, -gate, s

slum — my, s

slumber — ed, ing, er, s

slump — ed, ing, s

slung

slunk

slush — ed, ing, es

slush y — ier, iest, iness

sly — er, est, ly, ness

sm

smack — ed, ing, s

small — er, est, ness

smart — ed, ing, er, est, ly, ness, s

smarten — ed, ing, s

smash — ed, ing, es

smear — ed, ing, y, s

smell — ed, ing, er, s

smell y — ier, iest, iness

smelt or smelled

smile — d, ⌀ing, r, s

smirk — ed, ing, er, s

smithereens

smock — ed, ing, s

smoke — d, ⌀ing, r, /bomb, /screen, s

smok y — ier, iest, ily, iness

smooth — ed, ing, er, est, ly, ness, s

smother — ed, ing, s

smoulder — ed, ing, s

smudge — d, ⌀ing, s

smudg y — ier, iest, iness

smuggle — d, ⌀ing, r, s

sn

snack — /bar, s

snag — ged, ging, s

snail — s

snake — d, ⌀ing, ⌀y, bite, -charmer, skin, s

snap — ped, ping, per, shot, s

snare — d, ⌀ing, r, s

snarl — ed, ing, er, s

snatch — ed, ing, es

sneak — ed, ing, er, s

sneak y — ier, iest, ily, iness

sneer — ed, ing, er, s

sneeze — d, ⌀ing, r, s

* sloe
  slow

sniff	ed, ing, er, s	**soften**	ed, ing, er, s
sniffle	d, ǿing, r, s	**sogg**y	ier, iest, ily, iness
snigger	ed, ing, er, s	**soil**	ed, ing, s
snip	ped, ping, per, s	**sold*** (sell)	
snipe	d, ǿing, r, s	**solder**	ed, ing, s
snivel	led, ling, ler, s	**soldier**	ed, ing, s
snob	bery, bish, bishness, s	**sole*** (only one; single)	ly
snooker	ed, ing, /ball, /player, /table, s	**sole*** (bottom of shoe, etc)	d*, ǿing, s
snooze	d, ǿing, s	**sole*** (fish)	s
snore	d, ǿing, r, s	**solemn**	ity, ly, ess
snorkel	led, ling, ler, s	**solicitor**	s
snort	ed, ing, er, s	**solid**	ity, ly, s
snow	ed, ing, drift, fall, flake, storm, s	**solitary**	
snow	man, men, plough, drop, shoe, s	**solo**	ist, s
snowball	ed, ing, s	**solution**	s
snowy	ier, iest, iness	**solve**	d, ǿing, r, s
snub	bed, bing, s	**some***	body, one, how, thing, where
snug	ger, gest, ly, ness	**sometime**	s
snuggle	d, ǿing, s	**somersault**	ed, ing, s
		son* (boy)	ny, s
SO		**song**	ster, /book, /bird, /sheet, /writer, s
soak	ed, ing, er, s	**soon**	er, est
soap	ed, ing, suds, /bubble, flakes, s	**soot**	y
soapy	ier, iest, ily, iness	**soothe**	d, ǿing, s
soar* (fly upwards)	ed, ing, s	**sopping**	/wet
sob	bed, bing, s	**sorcerer**	s
soccer		**sore*** (painful)	r, st, ly, ness, s
sociable	ǿy	**sorrow**	ed, ing, ful, fully, s
social	ly, s	**sorr**y	ier, iest, iness
socialist	s	**sort**	ed, ing, er, s
society	ies	**soul*** (spirit)	ful, fully, s
sock	s	**sound**	ed, ing, er, est, ly, ness, s
socket	s	**soup**	/plate, /spoon, s
soda	/bread, /water, s	**sour**	ed, ing, er, est, ly, ness, s
sodden		**source**	s
sofa	s	**south**	-east, -west, ern, erly, ward
soft	er, est, ish, ly, ness, -hearted, ware	**souvenir**	s

sovereign	s
sow* (scatter seed)	ed, ing, er, s
sown* (planted)	

sp

space	d, ∅ing, r, s, craft, man, woman
space	/capsule, ship, /shuttle, /station, s
spacious	ly, ness
spade	ful, s
spaghetti	
span	ned, ning, s
spangle	d, ∅ing, s
spaniel	s
spank	ed, ing, s
spanner	s
spare	d, ∅ing, /part, -time, /tyre, s
spark	ed, ing, s
sparkle	d, ∅ing, r, s
sparrow	hawk, s
sparse	∅ity, ly, ness
spat	
spawn	ed, ing, s
speak	ing, er, s
spear	ed, ing, man, men, head, gun, s
special	ly, ty, ist, ity
specialize	d, ∅ing, ∅ation, s
specimen	s
speck	ed, ing, less, s
speckle	d, ∅ing, s
spectacle	s
spectacular	ly
spectator	s
spectre	s
sped or speeded	
speech	/day, less, es
speed	ed, ing, boat, /limit, way, s
speed y	ier, iest, ily, iness

spell	ed, ing, er, binding, bound, s
spelt or spelled	
spend	ing, er, thrift, s
spent	
sphere	s
spider	y, s
spied	
spike	d, ∅ing, s
spill	ed, ing, s
spilt or spilled	
spin	ning, ner, -dryer, s
spinach	
spinster	s
spiral	led, ling, ly, s
spire	s
spirit	ed, ing, /level, s
spit	ting, ter, s
spite	d, ∅ing, s
spiteful	ly, ness
splash	ed, ing, es
splendid	ly
splendour	s
splint	s
splinter	ed, ing, y, s
split	ting, ter, s
splutter	ed, ing, er, s
spoil	ed, ing, er, sport, s
spoilt or spoiled	
spoke (speak)	n, sman, swoman
spoke (of wheel)	s
sponge	d, ∅ing, ∅y, r, /bag, /cake, s
sponsor	ed, ing, s
spontaneous	ly
spook y	ier, iest, ily, iness
spoon	ed, ing, ful, s
sport	ed, ing, s, sman, swoman
sport y	ier, iest, ily, iness

*	sow sown
	sew sewn
	so

spot	*ted, ting, ter, less, lessly, light, s*
spott *y*	*ier, iest, ily, iness*
spout	*ed, ing, s*
sprain	*ed, ing, s*
sprang	
sprawl	*ed, ing, er, s*
spray	*ed, ing, er, s*
spread	*ing, er, sheet, s*
sprightl *y*	*ier, iest, iness*
spring	*ing, -cleaning, board, time, s*
spring *y*	*ier, iest, ily, iness*
sprinkle	*d, ✗ing, r, s*
sprint	*ed, ing, er, s*
sprout	*ed, ing, s*
sprung	
spun	
spurt	*ed, ing, s*
spy	*ing*
sp *ied*	*ies*

sq

squabble	*d, ✗ing, r, s*
squad	*ron, s*
squall	*ed, ing, y, s*
squander	*ed, ing, er, s*
square	*d, ✗ing, ly, ness, /dance, root, s*
squash	*ed, ing, y, es*
squat	*ted, ting, ter, s*
squaw	*s*
squawk	*ed, ing, er, s*
squeak	*ed, ing, er, s*
squeak *y*	*ier, iest, ily, iness*
squeal	*ed, ing, er, s*
squeeze	*d, ✗ing, r, s*
squelch	*ed, ing, es*
squib	*s*
squint	*ed, ing, er, s*

squire	*s*
squirm	*ed, ing, er, s*
squirrel	*s*
squirt	*ed, ing, er, s*

st

stab	*bed, bing, ber, s*
stable	*d, ✗ing, /boy, /girl, s*
stack	*ed, ing, s*
stadium	*s* or **stadia**
staff	*ed, ing, room, s*
stag	*hound, /hunt, s*
stage	*d, ✗ing, hand, /manager, s*
stagecoach	*es*
stagger	*ed, ing, er, s*
stain	*ed, ing, less, er, s*
stair*	*case, lift, -rod, way, s*
stake* (a stick; bet)	*d, ✗ing, s*
stale	*r, st, ly, ness*
stalk	*ed, ing, er, s*
stall	*ed, ing, holder, s*
stallion	*s*
stamina	
stammer	*ed, ing, er, s*
stamp	*ed, ing, /album, /collector, s*
stampede	*d, ✗ing, s*
stand	*ing, still, s*
standard	*-bearer, s*
star	*red, ring, less, light, lit, s*
starr *y*	*ier, iest, ily, iness*
starboard	
starfish	*es* or **starfish**
starch	*ed, ing, es*
stare* (look at)	*d, ✗ing, r, s*
starling	*s*
start	*ed, ing, er, s*
startle	*d, ✗ing, s*

*	stair	stake
	stare	steak

starve	d, ∅ing, ∅ation, s
state	d, ∅ing, ment, s
stately	ier, iest, iness
station	ed, ing, /master, s
stationary* (still; not moving)	
stationer	s
stationery* (paper, pens, etc)	
statue	tte, s
staunch	ed, ing, er, est, ly, ness, es
stay	ed, ing, er, s
steady	ing
steadied	ier, iest, ily, iness, ies
steak* (meat)	s
steal* (thieve)	ing, s
stealth	
stealthy	ier, iest, ily, iness
steam	ed, ing, er, /engine, ship, s
steamy	ier, iest, ily, iness
steel* (metal)	ed, ing, y, /band, /drum, s
steep	er, est, ly, ness
steeple	chase, jack, s
steer	age, ed, ing, er, sman, smen, s
steering wheel	s
stem	med, ming, s
stencil	led, ling, ler, s
step	ped, ping, ladder, s
step	father, mother, brother, sister, s
stepping stone	s
stereophonic	
sterilize	d, ∅ing, ∅ation, r, s
stern	er, est, ly, ness
stew	ed, ing, er, s
steward	s
stewardess	es
stick	ing, er, /insect, s
sticky	ier, iest, ily, iness
stickleback	s

stiff	er, est, ly, ness
stiffen	ed, ing, er, s
stifle	d, ∅ing, r, s
stile* (steps)	s
still	ed, ing, ness, s
sting	ing, er, s
stinging nettle	s
stir	red, ring, rer, s
stirrup	s
stitch	ed, ing, es
stoat	s
stock	ed, ing, ist, -car, pile, room, s
stocking	s
stoke	d, ∅ing, r, s
stole	n
stomach	-ache, /pump, s
stone	d, ∅ing, -cold, -deaf, mason, s
stony	ier, iest, ily, iness
stood	
stool	s
stoop	ed, ing, s
stop	ped, ping, pable, page, per, gap, s
store	d, ∅ing, ∅age, house, room, s
storey* (floor)	s
stork	s
storm	ed, ing, /cloud, s
stormy	ier, iest, ily, iness
story* (tale)	ies
stout	er, est, ly, ness, ish, -hearted
stove	-pipe, s
stow	ed, ing, away, s
straggle	d, ∅ing, r, s
straight* (not bent)	er, est, forward
straighten	ed, ing, er, s
strain	ed, ing, er, s
strait* (sea channel)	s
strand	ed, ing, s

---

strange	r, st, ly, ness	stud	ded, ding, s
stranger	s	student	s
strangle	d, øing, hold, r, s	studio	s
strap	ped, ping, less, s	studious	ly, ness
straw	/hat, s	study	ing
strawberr y	ies	stud ied	ies
stray	ed, ing, er, s	stuff	ed, ing, er, s
streak	ed, ing, er, s	stuff y	ier, iest, ily, iness
streak y	ier, iest, ily, iness	stumble	d, øing, r, s
stream	ed, ing, lined, er, s	stump	ed, ing, y, s
street	/lighting, /sweeper, s	stun	ned, ning, ner, s
strength	s	stung	
strengthen	ed, ing, er, s	stunt	ed, ing, man, woman, s
strenuous	ly, ness	stupendous	ly, ness
stretch	ed, ing, es	stupid	er, est, ity, ly
stretcher	-bearer, s	sturd y	ier, iest, ily, iness
stricken		stutter	ed, ing, er, s
strict	er, est, ly, ness	st y	ies
stride	øing, r, s	style* (way; fashion)	d, øing, øish, øist, s
strike	øing, r, s		
string	ing, s		su
strip	ped, ping, per, -lighting, s	subject	ed, ing, s
stripe	d, øing, s	submarine	r, s
strode		submerge	d, øing, s
stroke	d, øing, r, s	submit	ted, ting, s
stroll	ed, ing, er, s	subscribe	d, øing, r, s
strong	er, est, ly, ish, hold, room	subscription	s
struck		subside	d, øing, nce, s
structure	s	substance	s
struggle	d, øing, r, s	substantial	ly
strum	med, ming, mer, s	substitute	d, øing, øion, s
strung		subtract	ed, ing, ion, s
strut	ted, ting, ter, s	suburb	s
stub	bed, bing, by, s	succeed	ed, ing, s
stubble		success	es
stubborn	ly, ness	successful	ly
stuck		succession	s

* style
 stile

successor	*s*	**supermarket**	*s*
such	*like*	**superstition**	*s*
suck	*ed, ing, er, s*	**superstitious**	*ly, ness*
suction	*/pump*	**supervise**	*d, ȼing, ȼion, ȼor, s*
sudden	*ly, ness*	**supper**	*time, s*
sue	*d, ȼing, s*	**supple**	*r, st, ness*
suede	*s*	**supplement**	*s*
suet	*/pudding, y*	**supply**	*ing*
suffer	*ed, ing, er, s*	**suppl**ied	*ier, ies*
sufficient	*ly*	**support**	*ed, ing, er, s*
suffocate	*d, ȼing, ȼion, s*	**suppose**	*d, ȼing, s*
sugar *ed, ing, y, /basin, /beet, /cane, s*		**supreme**	*ly*
suggest	*ed, ing, ion, s*	**sure*** (certain)	*r, st, ly, ness, -footed*
suicide	*ȼal, s*	**surf*** (sea foam)	*ing, board, -riding, er, s*
suit *ed, ing, able, ably, ability, case, s*		**surface**	*d, ȼing, s*
suite* (set of furniture, rooms, etc)	*s*	**surge**	*d, ȼing, s*
sulk	*ed, ing, s*	**surgeon**	*s*
sulky	*ier, iest, ily, iness*	**surger**y	*ies*
sullen	*ly, ness*	**surname**	*s*
sultana	*s*	**surpass**	*ed, ing, es*
sum* (add up; total)	*med, ming, s*	**surplice*** (gown)	*s*
summer	*y, time, /house, s*	**surplus*** (left over)	*es*
summit	*s*	**surprise**	*d, ȼing, s*
summon	*ed, ing, s*	**surrender**	*ed, ing, s*
sumptuous	*ly, ness*	**surround**	*ed, ing, s*
sun* *ned, ning, beam, light, flower, s*		**survey**	*ed, ing, or, s*
sun* *glasses, rise, set, shine, shade, s*		**survive**	*d, ȼing, ȼal, ȼor, s*
sunny	*ier, iest, ily, iness*	**suspect**	*ed, ing, s*
sunbathe	*d, ȼing, r, s*	**suspend**	*ed, ing, er, s*
sunburn	*ed, t*	**suspense**	
sundae* (ice cream)	*s*	**suspicion**	*s*
Sunday*	*/school, s*	**suspicious**	*ly, ness*
sung		**sustain**	*ed, ing, s*
sunk	*en*		
superb	*ly*		**SW**
superintend	*ed, ing, ent, s*	**swagger**	*ed, ing, er, s*
superior	*ity, s*	**swallow**	*ed, ing, er, s*

*****	suite	sum	sun	sundae	
	sweet	some	son	Sunday	
*****	sure	surf	surplice		
	shore	serf	surplus		

swam	
swamp	ed, ing, y, s
swan	s
swank	ed, ing, y, s
swap or swop	ped, ping, per, s
swarm	ed, ing, s
swarth y	ier, iest, ily, iness
swat	ted, ting, ter, s
sway	ed, ing, s
swear	ing, er, -word, s
sweat	ed, ing, y, er, band, shirt, suit, s
swede	s
sweep	ing, er, stake, s
swept	
sweet*	er, est, ish, ly, ness, heart, /pea, s
sweeten	ed, ing, er, s
swell	ed, ing, s
swelter	ed, ing, s
swept	
swerve	d, ⌀ing, s
swift	er, est, ly, ness, s
swill	ed, ing, s
swim	mer, suit, s
swimming	/bath, /pool, /trunks
swindle	d, ⌀ing, r, s
swine	herd, swine
swing	ing, er, s
swipe	d, ⌀ing, r, s
swirl	ed, ing, s
swish	ed, ing, es
switch	ed, ing, es
swivel	led, ling, s
swollen	
swoon	ed, ing, s
swoop	ed, ing, s
swop or swap	ped, ping, per, s
sword	sman, smen, s

swore	
sworn	
swot	ted, ting, s
swum	
swung	

sy

sycamore	/tree, s
syllable	s
syllabus	es
symbol	ic, s
sympathetic	ally
sympathize	d, ⌀ing, r, s
sympath y	ies
symphon y	ies
symptom	s
synagogue	s
syringe	d, ⌀ing, s
syrup	y
system	atic, atically, s

ta

tabby cat	s
table	cloth, -mat, /tennis, s
tablespoon	ful, s
tableau	x
tablet	s
tack	ed, ing, s
tackle	d, ⌀ing, r, s
tact	ful, fully, less, lessly
tactics	
tadpole	s
tag	ged, ging, s
tail*	ed, ing, back, -end, /light, spin, s
tailor	ed, ing, -made, s

* sweet / suite

* tail / tale

take	n, ∅ing, r, away, -off, s	tasteless	ly, ness
talcum powder		tatter	ed, s
tale* (story)	bearer, teller, s	tattoo	ed, ing, er, ist, s
talent	ed, s	taught* (teach)	
talk	ative, ed, ing, er, s	taunt	ed, ing, er, s
tall	er, est, ish, ness	taut* (tight)	er, est, ly, ness
Talmud		tavern	s
talon	s	tax	ation, ed, ing, es
tambourine	s	taxi	cab, /driver, /rank, s
tame	d, ∅ing, r, st, ly, ness, s		
tamper	ed, ing, er, s		

te

tan	ned, ning, ner, s	tea*	cake, cup, pot, time, s
tandem	s	tea*	/bag, /chest, /shop, /towel, s
tangerine	s	tea leaf	/leaves
tangle	d, ∅ing, s	tea part y	ies
tango	ed, ing, s	teaspoon	ful, s
tank	er, ful, s	teach	ing, ings, es
tankard	s	teacher	s
tantalize	d, ∅ing, s	teak	
tantrum	s	team* (side; number)	/leader, work, s
tap	ped, ping, per, -dance, -dancing, s	tear* (pull apart)	ing, s
tape	d, ∅ing, s	tear	/gas, drop, s
tape	-measure, /recorder, /recording, s	tearful	ly, ness
tapestr y	ies	tease	d, ∅ing, r, s
tapioca		technical	ly
tar	red, ring, ry, s	technician	s
tarantula	s	teddy bear	s
tare* (weed)	s	tedious	ly, ness
target	s	tee* (golf)	d, ing, /shot, s
tarnish	ed, ing, es	teem* (pour; swarm)	ed, ing, s
tarpaulin	s	teenage	d, /boy, /girl
tart	let, s	teenager	s
tartan	s	tee-shirt or T-shirt	s
task	ed, ing, master, s	teeth	
tassel	s	telegram	s
taste	d, ∅ing, ∅y, r, s	telegraph	ed, ing, /line, /pole, /wire, s
tasteful	ly, ness	telephone	d, ∅ing, /book, /number, s

---

* tale	tare	
tail	tear	

* taught	tea	team
taut	tee	teem

telescope	*d, ∅ing, s*		**th**	
televise	*d, ∅ing, s*	**than**	
television	*s*	**thank**	*ed, ing, s*
tell	*ing, er, -tale, s*	**thankful**	*ly, ness*
temper	*ed, ing, s*	**thankless**	*ly, ness*
temperature	*s*	**that**	
temple	*s*	**that's** (that is)	
temporar*y*	*ily*	**thatch**	*ed, ing, es*
tempt	*ation, ed, ing, er, s*	**thaw**	*ed, ing, s*
tend	*ed, ing, s*	**theatre**	*/ticket, s*
tender	*-hearted, ly, ness*	**theatrical**	*ly, s*
tenement	*s*	**theft**	*s*
tennis	*/ball, /court, /player, /racket*	**their*** (belonging to them)	
tenor	*s*	**theirs*** (belonging to them)	
tense	*d, ∅ing, r, st, ly, ness, s*	**them**	*selves*
tent	*/peg, /pole, /rope, s*	**theme**	*/park, s*
tentacle	*s*	**then**	
tepid	*ly, ness*	**theor***y*	*ies*
term	*ly, ed, ing, s*	**there*** (in that place)	*abouts, after*
terminate	*d, ∅ing, ∅ion, ∅or, s*	**therefore**	
terminus	*es or* **termini**	**there's*** (there is)	
terrace	*d, ∅ing, /house, s*	**thermometer**	*s*
terrible	*∅y, ness*	**Thermos flask**	*s*
terrier	*s*	**thesaurus**	*es*
terrific	*ally*	**these**	
terrify	*ing*	**they**	
terrif*ied*	*ies*	**they'll** (they will; they shall)	
territorial	*s*	**they're*** (they are)	
territor*y*	*ies*	**they've** (they have)	
terror	*ism, ist, -stricken, s*	**thick**	*er, est, ly, ness, ish, -skinned*
terrorize	*d, ∅ing, s*	**thicken**	*ed, ing, er, s*
test	*ed, ing, /paper, /pilot, /tube, s*	**thicket**	*s*
testament	*s*	**thief**	**thieves**
testimonial	*s*	**thieve**	*∅ing, s*
tether	*ed, ing, s*	**thimble**	*ful, s*
text	*ed, ing, book, /message, s*	**thin**	*ned, ning, ner, nest, ly, ness, s*
textile	*s*	**thing**	*s*

*****	their	theirs
	there	there's
	they're	

think	ing, er, s
thirst	ed, ing, s
thirst y	ier, iest, ily, iness
this	
thistle	s
thorn	s
thorn y	ier, iest, ily, iness
thorough	ly, ness, bred, fare
those	
though	
thought	-reader, s
thoughtful	ly, ness
thoughtless	ly, ness
thrash	ed, ing, es
thread	ed, ing, bare, er, s
threat	s
threaten	ed, ing, s
threw* (throw)	
thrift	less
thrift y	ier, iest, ily, iness
thrill	ed, ing, er, s
thrive	d, ⌀ing, s
throat	s
throb	bed, bing, s
throne* (king's or queen's seat)	s
throng	ed, ing, s
throttle	d, ⌀ing, s
through* (from end to end)	out, way
throw	n*, ing, er, s
thrush	es
thrust	ing, s
thud	ded, ding, s
thug	s
thumb	ed, ing, nail, print, screw, s
thump	ed, ing, er, s
thunder	ed, ing, y, bolt, clap, storm, s
Thursday	s

ti

tiara	s
tick	ed, ing, s
ticket	/collector, -holder, /office, s
tickle	d, ⌀ing, ⌀ish, r, s
tide* (sea)	mark, s
tidings	
tidy	ing
tid ied	ier, iest, ily, iness, ies
tie	d*, -clip, -pin, s
tying	
tiger	s
tigress	es
tight	er, est, ly, ness, rope, s
tighten	ed, ing, er, s
tile	d, ⌀ing, r, s
till	ed, ing, er, s
till or until	
tilt	ed, ing, er, s
timber	ed, /yard, s
time	d, ⌀ing, r, ly, less, /bomb, table, s
timid	ity, ly, ness
tin	ned, ning, ny, foil, -opener, -tack, s
tinge	d, ⌀ing, s
tingle	d, ⌀ing, s
tinker	ed, ing, s
tinkle	d, ⌀ing, s
tinsel	
tint	ed, ing, s
tin y	ier, iest, ily, iness
tip	ped, ping, per, ster, s
tiptoe	d, ing, s
tire* (weary)	d, ⌀ing, some, s
tireless	ly, ness
tissue	/paper, s
title	d, s
titter	ed, ing, s

threw throne
* through thrown

tide tire
* tied tyre

to

to* (towards)

toad	-in-the-hole, s
toadstool	s
to and fro	
toast	ed, ing, er, /rack, s
tobacco	nist, /pipe, /smoke, s
toboggan	ed, ing, er, s
today	
toddle	d, ẓing, r, s
toe*	d, ing, cap, hold, nail, s
toffee	/apple, /paper, s
toga	s
together	ness
toil	ed, ing, er, s
toilet	/paper, /roll, /soap, s
token	s
told	
tolerant	ly
tolerate	d, ẓing, ẓion, s
toll	ed, ing, /bridge, /gate, /road, s
tomahawk	s
tomato	es
tomb	stone, s
tomboy	s
tomcat	s
tomorrow	s
ton or tonne (metric)	s
tone	d, ẓing, -deaf, s
tongs	
tongue	-tied, -twister, s
tonic	s
tonight	
tonsil	s
tonsillitis	
too* (more than enough; also)	
took	

tool	/bag, /kit, /shed, s
tooth	ache, paste, powder, less, **teeth**
toothbrush	es
top	ped, ping, per, less, -heavy, /hat, s
topic	al, s
topple	d, ẓing, s
topsy-turvy	
Torah	
torch	es
tore	
torment	ed, ing, or, s
torn	
tornado	es
torpedo	ed, ing, es
torrent	ial, s
tortoise	shell, s
torture	d, ẓing, r, /chamber, s
toss	ed, ing, es
total	led, ling, ly, s
totter	ed, ing, y, er, s
touch	ed, ing, y, es
tough	er, est, ly, ness, s
toughen	ed, ing, s
tour	ed, ing, ism, ist, s
tournament	s
tow* (pull)	ed, ing, line, path, /rope, s
towards or toward	
towel	led, ling, /rail, s
tower	ed, ing, /block, s
town	/council, /crier, /hall, s
toy	ed, ing, shop, s

tr

trace	d, ẓing, able, r, s
tracing paper	
track	ed, ing, er, suit, s
tractor	/driver, s

* to   toe
  too   tow
  two (2)

trade	*d, ¢ing, mark, sman, swoman, r, s*	**tremendous**	*ly, ness*
tradition	*al, ally, s*	**trench**	*es*
traffic	*/jam, /lights, /signal, /warden*	**trend** *y*	*ier, iest, ily, iness*
traged *y*	*ies*	**trespass**	*ed, ing, es*
tragic	*ally*	**trespasser**	*s*
trail	*ed, ing, er, s*	**trestle**	*-table, s*
train	*ed, ing, er, s*	**trial**	*s*
traitor	*ous, ously, s*	**triangle**	*s*
tramp	*ed, ing, er, s*	**tribe**	*sman, smen, swoman, swomen, s*
trample	*d, ¢ing, r, s*	**tributar** *y*	*ies*
trampoline	*s*	**trick**	*ed, ing, ery, ster, s*
trance	*s*	**trick** *y*	*ier, iest, ily, iness*
transact	*ed, ing, ion, s*	**trickle**	*d, ¢ing, s*
transfer	*red, ring, able, s*	**tricycle**	*s*
transform	*ed, ing, ation, s*	**trifle**	*d, ¢ing, s*
transfusion	*s*	**trigger**	*ed, ing, s*
translate	*d, ¢ing, ¢ion, s*	**trim**	*med, ming, mer, mest, ly, ness, s*
transparent	*ly*	**trinket**	*s*
transport	*ed, ing, er, ation, able, s*	**trio**	*s*
trap	*ped, ping, per, door, s*	**trip**	*ped, ping, per, s*
trapeze	*s*	**triple**	*d, ¢ing, s*
trash	*ed, ing, es*	**triplet**	*s*
travel	*led, ling, ler, s*	**tripod**	*s*
trawl	*ed, ing, er, s*	**triumph**	*ed, ing, ant, antly, s*
tray	*ful, s*	**trod**	*den*
treacherous	*ly*	**trolley**	*s*
treacher *y*	*ies*	**trombone**	*¢ist, s*
treacle	*/tart, s*	**troop*** (of scouts, soldiers)	*ed, ing, er, s*
tread	*ing, s*	**troph** *y*	*ies*
treason	*able*	**tropic**	*al, ally, s*
treasure	*d, ¢ing, r, /chest, /hunt, s*	**trot**	*ted, ting, ter, s*
treat	*ed, ing, able, ment, s*	**trouble**	*d, ¢ing, some, maker, s*
treble	*d, ¢ing, s*	**trough**	*s*
tree	*/stump, top, /trunk, s*	**troupe*** (of entertainers)	*r, s*
trek	*ked, king, ker, s*	**trousers**	
trellis	*-work*	**trousseau**	*x or s*
tremble	*d, ¢ing, s*	**trout**	*-fishing,* **trout**

trowel	s	tunic	s
truant	ed, ing, s	tunnel	led, ling, ler, s
truck	/driver, load, s	turban	s
trudge	d, ∉ing, s	turbine	s
true	r, st, ness	turf	ed, ing, s or **turves**
truly		turkey	/cock, /hen, s
trumpet	ed, ing, er, s	**Turkish delight**	
truncheon	s	turmoil	s
trunk	s	turn	ed, ing, er, over, stile, table, s
truss	ed, ing, es	turnip	s
trust	ed, ing, worthy, s	turpentine	
trust y	ier, iest, ily, iness	turquoise	
truth	s	turret	ed, s
truthful	ly, ness	turtle	neck, /shell, -dove, s
try	ing	tusk	s
tr ied	ier, ies	tussle	d, ∉ing, s
		tutor	ial, s
tu		tutu	s

tubb y	ier, iest, iness		
tube	∉ing, /train, s	**tw**	
tuck	ed, ing, /shop, s	tweak	ed, ing, s
Tudor	s	tweed	s
Tuesday	s	tweezers	
tuft	s	twice	
tug	ged, ging, ger, boat, s	twiddle	d, ∉ing, r, s
tug of war		twig	s
tuition		twilight	
tulip	s	twin	ned, ning, /brother, /sister, s
tumble	d, ∉ing, r, down, -dryer, s	twine	d, ∉ing, s
tumbler	ful, s	twinge	d, ∉ing, s
tumult	s	twinkle	d, ∉ing, s
tumultuous	ly, ness	twirl	ed, ing, s
tuna	s or **tuna**	twist	ed, ing, er, s
tundra	s	twist y	ier, iest, ily, iness
tune	d, ∉ing, r, s	twitch	ed, ing, es
tuneful	ly, ness	twitter	ed, ing, s
tuneless	ly, ness	**two*** (2)	s

* two (2)
   too
   to

ty

tying
type   d, øing, øist, written, writing, writer, s
typhoon   s
typical   ly
tyrannize   d, øing, s
tyrant   s
tyre* (wheel cover)   s

ug

ugl y   ier, iest, iness

um

umbrella   s
umpire   d, øing, s

un

unable
unafraid
unaminous   ly
unarm   ed, ing, s
unattractive   ly, ness
unavoidable   øy
unaware   s
unbearable   øy
unbeaten
unbelievable   øy
unbolt   ed, ing, s
unbuckle   d, øing, s
unbutton   ed, ing, s
uncann y   ier, iest, ily, iness
uncertain   ly, ty
uncivilized
uncle   s
unclean   liness
uncomfortable   øy, ness

uncommon   ly, ness
unconscious   ly, ness
uncork   ed, ing, s
uncover   ed, ing, s
uncurl   ed, ing, s
undamaged
undecided   ly
under   clothes, clothing, wear
under   go, going, goes, gone, went
undercurrent   s
underground
undergrowth
underline   d, øing, s
underneath
understand   able, ing, s
understood
understudy   ing
understud ied   ies
undertake   n, øing, r, s
undertook
underwater
undid
undo   ing
undone
undoubted   ly
undress   ed, ing, es
uneas y   ier, iest, ily, iness
unemploy ed   ment
uneven   ly, ness
unexpected   ly, ness
unexplored
unfair   ly, ness
unfasten   ed, ing, s
unfinished
unfit   ness
unfold   ed, ing, s
unfortunate   ly

*   tyre
    tire

unfriendl*y*	*ier, iest, iness*	unsaddle	*d, ∉ing, s*
unfurnished		unsafe	*r, st, ly, ness*
ungrateful	*ly, ness*	unscrew	*ed, ing, s*
unguarded	*ly, ness*	unselfish	*ly, ness*
unhapp*y*	*ier, iest, ily, iness*	unstead*y*	*ier, iest, ily, iness*
unharmed		unsuitable	*∉y*
unhealth*y*	*ier, iest, ily, iness*	untangle	*d, ∉ing, s*
unhurt		untid*y*	*ier, iest, ily, iness*
uniform	*s*	untie	*d, s*
unimportant		untying	
uninhabited		until *or* till	
uninjured		untrue	
uninteresting		unusual	*ly, ness*
Union Jack	*s*	unwelcome	
unite	*d, ∉ing, s*	unwell	
universe	*∉al*	unwilling	*ly, ness*
universit*y*	*ies*	unwise	*ly*
unjust	*ly, ness*	unwrap	*ped, ping, s*
unkind	*er, est, ly, ness*		
unknown		**up**	
unlawful	*ly, ness*	upbringing	
unless		upheaval	*s*
unlike	*ness*	uphill	
unlikel*y*	*ier, iest, ihood*	upholster	*ed, ing, y, er, s*
unload	*ed, ing, s*	upkeep	
unlock	*ed, ing, s*	upon	
unluck*y*	*ier, iest, ily, iness*	upper	*most, -cut, s*
unmistakable	*∉y*	upright	*s*
unnecessar*y*	*ily*	uprising	*s*
unoccupied		uproar	*s*
unpack	*ed, ing, s*	uproot	*ed, ing, s*
unpleasant	*ly, ness*	upset	*ting, s*
unpopular	*ity, ly*	upside-down	
unravel	*led, ling, s*	upstairs	
unreasonable	*∉y*	upstream	
unreliab*le*	*ility*	upturn	*ed, ing, s*
unrul*y*	*ier, iest, iness*	upward	*ly, s*

ur

uranium	
urban	
urchin	s
urge	d, ∅ing, s
urgenc y	ies
urgent	ly
urn* (vase; tea-urn)	s

us

use	d, ∅ing, ∅able, ∅age, r, s
useful	ly, ness
useless	ly, ness
usher	ed, ing, s
usherette	s
usual	ly, ness

ut

utensil	s
utilize	d, ∅ing, ∅ation, s
utmost	
utter	ed, ing, ance, s
utter	ly, most

va

vacanc y	ies
vacant	ly
vacate	d, ∅ing, ∅ion, s
vaccinate	d, ∅ing, ∅ion, s
vaccine	s
vacuum	/cleaner, /flask, s
vague	r, st, ly, ness
vain* (proud)	er, est, ly
vale* (valley)	s
valentine	/card, s
valiant	ly

valley	s
valuable	s
value	d, ∅ing, less, r, s
valve	s
vandal	s
vandalize	d, ∅ing, s
vane* (weathercock)	s
vanilla	
vanish	ed, ing, es
vanit y	ies
vanquish	ed, ing, es
vaporize	d, ∅ing, s
vapour	s
variet y	ies
various	ly, ness
varnish	ed, ing, es
vary	ing
var ied	ies
vase	s
Vaseline	
vast	er, est, ly, ness
vault	ed, ing, er, s

ve

veal	
Veda (Hindu holy book)	s
veer	ed, ing, s
vegetable	s
vegetarian	s
vegetation	
vehicle	s
veil* (a head or face covering)	ed, ing, s
vein* (blood vessel)	ed, ing, s
velvet	y, s
vengeance	
venison	
vent	ed, ing, -hole, s

---

*	urn	vain	vale
	earn	vane	veil
		vein	

ventilate	d, ∅ing, ∅ion, ∅or, s
ventriloquist	s
venture	d, ∅ing, some, s
veranda	s
verb	al, ally, s
verdict	s
verge	d, ∅ing, s
verger	s
verif y	ied, ing, ies
vermin	ous
versatile	∅ity
verse	s
version	s
versus	
vertical	ly
very	
vessel	s
vest	s
vestibule	s
vestr y	ies
vet	ted, ting, s
veteran	s
veterinar y	ies
vex	ed, ing, es, ation, atious

vi

viaduct	s
vibrate	d, ∅ing, ∅ion, s
vicar	age, s
vice	/admiral, /captain, s
vicinit y	ies
vicious	ly, ness
victim	s
victimize	d, ∅ing, ∅ation, s
Victorian	s
victor y	ious, ies
video	/game, /recorder, /tape, s

view	d, ∅ing, er, point, s
vigilant	
vigorous	ly
vigour	
Viking	s
vile	r, st, ly, ness
villa	s
village	r, s
villain* (scoundrel)	ous, s
villein* (serf)	s
vine	yard, s
vinegar	y
viola	s
violence	
violent	ly
violet	s
violin	ist, s
virtual	ly, /reality
virus	es
visible	∅y
visibility	
vision	s
visit	ed, ing, or, s
vital	ity, ly
vivid	ly, ness
vixen	s

vo

vocabular y	ies
vocal	ist, s
voice	d, ∅ing, s
volcano	es
vole	s
volley	ed, ing, ball, s
volt	age, s
volume	s
voluntar y	ily

villain
* villein

volunteer	ed, ing, s
vomit	ed, ing, s
vote	d, ∅ing, r, s
vouch	ed, ing, es
voucher	s
vow	ed, ing, s
vowel	s
voyage	d, ∅ing, r, s

vu

vulgar	ity, ly
vulnerab *le*	ility
vulture	s

wa

waddle	d, ∅ing, r, s
wade	d, ∅ing, r, s
wafer	s
waft	ed, ing, er, s
wag	ged, ging, ger, s
wage	d, ∅ing, r, /earner, /packet, s
waggle	d, ∅ing, r, s
wagon	load, /wheel, s
waif	s
wail	ed, ing, er, s
waist* (middle of body)	coat, s
wait* (stay; serve)	ed, ing, s
waiter	s
waitress	es
waiting room	s
wake	d, ∅ing, r, s
waken	ed, ing, er, s
walk	ed, ing, er, s
wall	ed, ing, chart, flower, paper, s
wallet	s
wallow	ed, ing, er, s

walnut	/tree, s
walrus	es
waltz	ed, ing, es
wand	s
wander	ed, ing, er, s
wangle	d, ∅ing, r, s
want	ed, ing, s
war*	fare, head, paint, path, ship, s
warrior	s
warble	d, ∅ing, r, s
ward	ed, ing, en, er, s
wardrobe	s
ware* (goods)	house, s
warm	th, ed, ing, er, est, ish, ly, s
warn* (be careful)	ed, ing, er, s
warp	ed, ing, s
warrant	ed, ing, s
warren	s
warrior	s
wart	s
war *y*	ier, iest, ily, iness
wash	able, ed, ing, es
washer	s
wasn't (was not)	
wasp	s
waste*	d, ∅ing, land, /bin, /paper, /pipe, s
wasteful	ly, ness
watch	ed, ing, man, men, es
watchful	ly, ness
water	ed, ing, colour, cress, fall, proof, s
water *y*	ier, iest, iness
wave	d, ∅ing, s
waver	ed, ing, er, s
wav *y*	ier, iest, ily, iness
wax	ed, ing, en, es, works
wax *y*	ier, iest, ily, iness
way* (direction; manner; road)	lay, side, s

---

we

weak* (not strong)	*er, est, ly, ness, -kneed*
weaken	*ed, ing, s*
weakling	*s*
wealth	
wealth *y*	*ier, iest, ily, iness*
weapon	*s*
wear* (dressed in)	*ing, er, s*
weary	*ing*
wear *ied*	*ier, iest, ily, iness, ies*
weasel	*s*
weather*	*ed, ing, cock, /forecast, vane, s*
weave	*d, ∅ing, r, s*
web	*bed, bing, s*
web	*cam, cast, /page, site*
we'd (we had; we should; we would)	
wed	*ded, ding, s*
wedding	*/cake, /card, /day, /ring, s*
wedding dress	*es*
wedge	*d, ∅ing, s*
Wednesday	*s*
weed	*ed, ing, er, killer, s*
weed *y*	*ier, iest, iness*
week* (seven days)	*day, end, s*
weekl *y*	*ies*
weep	*ing, y, er, s*
wept	
weigh* (measure heaviness)	*ed, ing, s*
weight* (heaviness)	*ed, ing, -lifter, s*
weight *y*	*ier, iest, ily, iness*
weir	*s*
weird	*er, est, ly, ness*
welcome	*d, ∅ing, s*
weld	*ed, ing, er, s*
welfare	
well	*-behaved, -bred, -wisher, s*
we'll (we shall; we will)	

wellington boot	*s*
went	
wept	
we're (we are)	
were	
weren't (were not)	
west	*ern, erly, ward, wards*
wet	*ted, ting, ter, test, ly, ness, suit, s*
we've (we have)	

wh

whack	*ed, ing, s*
whale	*∅ing, r, bone, -boat, s*
wharf	*s* or **wharves**
what	*ever, soever*
what's (what is)	
wheat	*-field, -flour, germ, meal, s*
wheedle	*d, ∅ing, r, s*
wheel	*ed, ing, er, barrow, chair, s*
wheeze	*d, ∅ing, s*
whelk	*/stall, s*
when	*ever*
whence	
where	*abouts, as, by, fore, upon*
wherever	
whether* (if)	
which* (what one?; who?)	*ever*
whiff	*ed, ing, s*
while	*d, ∅ing, s*
whilst	
whimper	*ed, ing, er, s*
whine* (cry; wail)	*d, ∅ing, r, s*
whip	*ped, ping, per, s*
whippet	*s*
whirl	*ed, ing, igig, pool, wind, s*
whirr	*ed, ing, s*
whisk	*ed, ing, er, s*

*	weak	wear	weather	weigh	weight	*	which	whine
	week	ware	whether	way	wait		witch	wine

whisker	*ed, y, s*	wilderness	*es*
whisk*y*	*ies*	wilful	*ly, ness*
whisper	*ed, ing, er, s*	will	*ed, ing, -power, s*
whist	*/drive*	willing	*ly, ness*
whistle	*d, ∅ing, r, -blower, s*	willow	*/tree, s*
white	*r, st, ly, ness, board, s*	wil*y*	*ier, iest, ily, iness*
whiten	*ed, ing, er, s*	win	*ning, ner, s*
whitewash	*ed, ing, es*	wince	*d, ∅ing, s*
whiting	**whiting**	wind (turn; twist)	*ing, er, s*
Whit Sunday	*s*	wind	*ed, ing, fall, mill, surfer, ward, s*
Whitsun	*tide*	wind*y*	*ier, iest, ily, iness*
whizz	*ed, ing, es*	window	*/cleaner, /ledge, -pane, sill, s*
who	*ever*	windscreen	*/wiper, s*
who'd (who had; who would)		wine* (a drink)	*/bar, /bottle, /list, s*
who'll (who will; who shall)		wing	*ed, ing, er, span, s*
who's* (who is; who has)		wink	*ed, ing, er, s*
whom	*soever*	winkle	*d, ∅ing, r, s*
whole* (all; complete)	*sale, some*	winter	*ed, ing, time, s*
wholly* (completely)		wintr*y*	*ier, iest, ily, iness*
whoop	*ed, ing, s*	wipe	*d, ∅ing, r, s*
whose* (belonging to whom)		wire	*d, ∅ing, -netting, /rope, -cutter, s*
why		wireless	*es*
		wir*y*	*ier, iest, ily, iness*
		wisdom	*/tooth, /teeth*
## wi		wise	*r, st, ly*
wicked	*er, est, ly, ness*	wish	*ed, ing, es*
wicker	*work*	wishful	*ly, ness*
wicket	*keeper, s*	wistful	*ly, ness*
wide	*r, st, ly, spread, s*	wit	*ted, less, s*
widen	*ed, ing, er, s*	witt*y*	*ier, iest, ily, iness*
width	*s*	witch* (woman using magic)	*craft, es*
widow	*ed, ing, er, s*	with	*in, out*
wield	*ed, ing, er, s*	withdraw	*al, ing, n, s*
wife	*ly,* **wives**	withdrew	
wiggle	*d, ∅ing, r, s*	wither	*ed, ing, s*
wigwam	*s*	withstand	*ing, s*
wiki		withstood	
wild	*er, est, ly, ness, life, fowl, fire, s*		

---

*	who's	whole	wholly	
	whose	hole	holy	

*	wine	witch	
	whine	which	

witness	*ed, ing, /box, es*	wouldn't (would not)	
wizard	*ry, s*	wound (turned; twisted)	
wizened		wound (injure)	*ed, ing, s*
		wove	*n*

wo

wobble	*d, ∅ing, r, s*
woe	*begone, s*
woeful	*ly, ness*
woke	*n*
wolf	*/cub, /pack,* **wolves**
woman	*hood, ly,* **women**
won* (win)	
wonder	*ed, ing, ment, land, s*
wonderful	*ly, ness*
won't (will not)	
wood*	*ed, carver, cutter, land, work, s*
wooden	*ly, ness*
wood *louse*	*lice*
woodpecker	*s*
wool	*s*
woollen	*s*
wooll *y*	*ier, iest, iness, ies*
word	*ed, ing, /processor, s*
wore* (wear)	
work	*ed, ing, man, men, out, shop, er, s*
world	*-famous, wide, s*
worm	*ed, ing, y, -eaten, -cast, -hole, s*
worn* (wear)	*/out*
worry	*ing*
worr *ied*	*ier, ies, isome*
worse	
worsen	*ed, ing, s*
worst	
worship	*ped, ping, per, s*
worth	*less, while*
worth *y*	*ier, iest, ily, iness*
would* (past of will)	

wr

wrangle	*d, ∅ing, r, s*
wrap* (cover)	*ped, ping, per, s*
wrath	*ful, fully*
wreath	*s*
wreck	*age, ed, ing, er, s*
wren	*s*
wrench	*ed, ing, es*
wrestle	*d, ∅ing, r, s*
wretch	*es*
wretched	*ly, ness*
wriggle	*d, ∅ing, r, s*
wring* (twist)	*ing, er, s*
wrinkle	*d, ∅ing, ∅y, s*
wrist	*let, band, s*
write* (form letters)	*r, s*
writing	*/case, /desk, /paper, /table, s*
written	
writhe	*d, ∅ing, s*
wrong	*ed, ing, ful, ly, ness, s*
wrote	
wrung* (twisted)	
wry	*er, est, ly, ness*

x

X-ray	*ed, ing, s*
xylophone	*s*

ya

yacht	*ing, sman, swoman, -club, /race, s*
yank	*ed, ing, s*

---

yap	*ped, ping, per, s*
yard	*age, stick, s*
yarn	*ed, ing, s*
yawn	*ed, ing, s*

ye

year	*ly, ling, s*
yearn	*ed, ing, s*
yeast	*y*
yell	*ed, ing, er, s*
yellow	*er, est, ness, ish, y, s*
yeoman	*men*
yes	*es*
yesterday	*s*
yet	
yeti	*s*
yew*	*/tree, s*

yi

yield	*ed, ing, s*

yo

yodel	*led, ling, ler, s*
yoga	
yoghurt	
yoke* (wooden bar; join)	*d, ₵ing, s*
yokel	*s*
yolk* (of egg)	*s*
yonder	
Yorkshire pudding	*s*
you* (person)	
you'd (you had; you would)	
you'll (you will)	
you're* (you are)	
you've (you have)	

young	*er, est, ish*
youngster	*s*
your* (belonging to you)	
yours	
yourself	*selves*
youth	*/club, /hostel, s*
youthful	*ly, ness*
yowl	*ed, ing, er, s*

za

zap	*ped, ping, s*

ze

zeal	
zealous	*ly*
zebra	*/crossing, s*
zero	*/hour, s*
zest	*ful, fully*

zi

zigzag	*ged, ging, s*
zinc	
zip	*ped, ping, per, /fastener, s*
zither	*s*

zo

zodiac	
zombie	*s*
zone	*d, ₵ing, s*
zoo	*keeper, s*
zoologist	*s*
zoology	
zoom	*ed, ing, s*

zu

Zulu	*s*

---

* yew   yoke   you're
   you   yolk   your
   ewe

Girls' names

A
Abbie
Abby
Abigail
Adele
Adrienne
Aileen
Aimee
Alexandra
Alexis
Alice
Alicia
Alisha
Alison
Amanda
Amber
Amelia
Amy
Andrea
Angela
Anita
Ann(e)
Anna
Annabel
Annette
Anthea
Antonia
April
Ashley
Audrey
Avril

B
Barbara
Belinda
Beryl
Beth
Bethany
Betty
Beverley
Blanche
Brenda
Bridget
Brooke
Bryony

C
Caitlin
Cara
Carla
Carol(e)
Caroline
Carolyn
Carrie
Catherine
Cecilia
Celia
Charlotte
Charmaine
Chelsea
Cheryl
Chloe
Christine
Claire
Clare
Claudia
Colette
Corinne
Courtney

D
Daisy
Danielle
Daphne
Dawn
Debbie
Deborah
Debra
Deirdre
Delia
Denise
Diana
Diane
Donna
Dorothy

E
Eileen
Elaine
Eleanor
Elizabeth
Ella
Ellen
Ellie
Eloise
Emily
Emma
Enid
Erin
Estelle
Esther
Eve
Eveline
Evelyn
Evie

F
Faith
Fay(e)
Felicity
Fiona
Fleur
Frances
Francesca
Freya

G
Gabrielle
Gail
Gayle
Gaynor
Gemma
Georgia
Georgina
Geraldine
Germaine
Gillian
Gina
Glenda
Glynis
Grace
Gwyneth

H
Hannah
Harriet
Hayley
Hazel
Heather
Heidi
Helen

Hilary
Holly

I
Imogen
Irene
Iris
Isabel
Isabella
Isabelle
Isobel

J
Jacqueline
Jade
Jane
Janet
Janice
Janine
Jasmine
Jayne
Jean
Jeanette
Jennifer
Jessica
Jill
Joan
Joanna
Joanne
Jocelyn
Jodie
Johanna
Josephine
Joy
Judith
Julia

Julie
June
Justine

K
Karen
Kate
Katharine
Katherine
Kathleen
Katie
Katrina
Katy
Kay
Kayleigh
Keeley
Keira
Kelly
Kerry
Kimberly
Kirsten
Kirsty

L
Lara
Laura
Lauren
Leah
Leanne
Lesley
Libby
Lily
Linda
Lindsey
Lisa
Lorna
Lorraine
Louisa

Louise
Lucy
Lydia
Lyndsey
Lynn(e)

M
Madeleine
Madison
Maisie
Mandy
Margaret
Maria
Marie
Martina
Mary
Matilda
Maureen
Maxine
Megan
Melanie
Melinda
Melissa
Merle
Mia
Michelle
Millie
Milly
Miranda
Molly
Morgan

N
Nadia
Nadine
Nancy
Naomi
Natalie

Natasha
Niamh
Nichola
Nicola
Nicole
Nina

O
Olivia

P
Paige
Pamela
Patricia
Paula
Pauline
Penelope
Penny
Philippa
Phoebe
Polly
Poppy

R
Rachael
Rachel
Rebecca
Rebekah
Rita
Rosalie
Rosalind
Rosamund
Rose
Rosemary
Rosie
Rowena
Ruby
Ruth

S
Sadie
Sally
Sallyann
Samantha
Sandra
Sara(h)
Scarlett
Shannon
Sharon
Sheila
Shelley
Shirley
Shona
Sonia
Sophia
Sophie
Stacey
Stella
Stephanie
Susan
Susannah
Susanne
Suzanne
Sybil
Sylvia

T
Tamara
Tammy
Tamsin
Tania
Tanya
Tara
Teresa
Theresa
Tia
Tina

Tracey
Tracy

U
Una
Ursula

V
Valerie
Vanessa
Vicki
Vicky
Victoria
Virginia
Vivien
Vivienne

W
Wendy

Y
Yolande
Yvonne

Z
Zara
Zelda
Zeta
Zoe

Boys' names

A

Aaron
Adam
Adrian
Aidan
Alan
Alasdair
Alex
Alexander
Alfie
Alfred
Alistair
Allan
Andrew
Angus
Anthony
Antony
Archie
Arthur

B

Bailey
Barry
Ben
Benjamin
Bernard
Billy
Bradley
Brandon
Brendan
Brian
Bruce
Bryan

C

Callum
Calum
Calvin
Cameron
Carl
Cedric
Charles
Charlie
Chris
Christian
Christopher
Clifford
Clive
Colin
Connor
Corey
Craig

D

Dale
Damian
Daniel
Darren
David
Dean
Declan
Dennis
Derek
Dominic
Donald
Duncan
Dylan

E

Edmund
Edward
Elliott
Ellis
Eric
Ethan
Ewan

F

Finlay
Francis
Frank
Freddie
Frederick

G

Gareth
Gary
Gavin
Geoffrey
George
Gordon
Graham
Gregory
Guy

H

Harley
Harrison
Harry
Harvey
Henry
Howard
Hugh

I

Ian
Isaac
Ivan

J

Jack
Jacob
Jake
James
Jamie
Jason
Jay
Jeffrey
Jeremy
Joe
Joel
John
Jonathan
Jordan
Joseph
Josh
Joshua
Julian
Justin

K

Kai
Karl
Keiran
Keith
Kenneth
Kevin
Kian
Kyle

L

Lance
Laurence
Lawrence
Lee
Leo
Leon
Leonard
Leslie
Lewis
Liam
Louis
Lucas
Luke

M

Malcolm
Marc
Marcus
Mark
Martin
Mason
Matthew
Maurice
Max
Melvin
Michael
Mohammed
Morgan
Muhammad

N

Nathan
Nathaniel
Neil

Neville
Nicholas
Nigel
Noah
Noel
Norman

O

Oliver
Oscar
Owen

P

Patrick
Paul
Peter
Philip
Piers

Q

Quentin

R

Ralph
Raymond
Reece
Reginald
Rhys
Richard
Riley
Robbie
Robert
Robin
Roderick
Rodney
Roger
Roland
Rolf

Ronald
Rory
Ross
Roy
Rupert
Russell
Ryan

S

Sam
Samuel
Scott
Sean
Sebastian
Shane
Shaun
Sidney
Simon
Spencer
Stanley
Stephen
Steven
Stewart
Stuart

T

Taylor
Terence
Terry
Theo
Thomas
Timothy
Toby
Tom
Tony
Trevor
Tristram
Tyler

V

Vernon
Victor
Vincent
Vivian

W

Wallace
Walter
Warren
Wayne
Wilfred
William
Winston

Z

Zachary
Zak

Some countries and their people

Country	Person	Country	Person
Afghanistan	Afghan	Central African	Central African
Albania	Albanian	Republic	
Algeria	Algerian	Chad	Chadian
Andorra	Andorran	Chile	Chilean
Angola	Angolan	China	Chinese
Argentina	Argentinian	Colombia	Colombian
Armenia	Armenian	Congo	Congolese
Australia	Australian	Costa Rica	Costa Rican
Austria	Austrian	Côte d'Ivoire	Ivorian
Azerbaijan	Azerbaijani	Croatia	Croat
		Cuba	Cuban
Bahamas	Bahamian	Cyprus	Cypriot
Bahrain	Bahraini	Czech Republic	Czech
Bangladesh	Bangladeshi		
Barbados	Barbadian	Democratic	Congolese
Belarus	Belarussian	Republic of Congo	
Belgium	Belgian	Denmark	Dane
Belize	Belizian	Djibouti	Djiboutian
Benin	Beninese	Dominica	Dominican
Bhutan	Bhutanese	Dominican	Dominican
Bolivia	Bolivian	Republic	
Bosnia and	Bosnian;	East Timor	Timorese
Herzegovina	Herzegovinan	Ecuador	Ecuadorean
Botswana	Botswanan	Egypt	Egyptian
Brazil	Brazilian	El Salvador	El Salvadorean
Britain	Briton	Equatorial Guinea	Equatorial Guinean
Brunei Darussalam	Bruneian	Eritrea	Eritrean
Bulgaria	Bulgarian	Estonia	Estonian
Burkina Faso	Burkinabé	Ethiopia	Ethiopian
Burma (now called	Burmese		
Myanmar)		Fiji	Fijian
Burundi	Burundian	Finland	Finn or Finnish
		France	French
Cambodia	Cambodian		
Cameroon	Cameroonian	Gabon	Gabonese
Canada	Canadian	Gambia	Gambian
Cape Verde	Cape Verdean	Georgia	Georgian

Country	Person	Country	Person
Germany	German	Luxembourg	Luxembourger
Ghana	Ghanaian		
Greece	Greek	Macedonia	Macedonian
Grenada	Grenadian	Madagascar	Malagasy
Guatemala	Guatemalan	Malawi	Malawian
Guinea	Guinean	Malaysia	Malaysian
Guinea-Bissau	Guinea-Bissauan	Maldives	Maldivian
Guyana	Guyanese	Mali	Malian
		Malta	Maltese
Haiti	Haitian	Mauritania	Mauritanian
Holland	Netherlander	Mauritius	Mauritian
Honduras	Honduran	Mexico	Mexican
Hungary	Hungarian	Moldova	Moldovan
		Monaco	Monégasque or Monacan
Iceland	Icelander		
India	Indian	Mongolia	Mongolian
Indonesia	Indonesian	Montenegro	Montenegrin
Iran	Iranian	Morocco	Moroccan
Iraq	Iraqi	Mozambique	Mozambican
Ireland	Irishman or Irishwoman	Myanmar	Myanmarese or Burmese
Israel	Israeli		
Italy	Italian	Namibia	Namibian
		Nepal	Nepalese or Nepali
Jamaica	Jamaican	Netherlands	Netherlander
Japan	Japanese	New Zealand	New Zealander
Jordan	Jordanian	Nicaragua	Nicaraguan
		Niger	Nigerien
Kazakhstan	Kazakhstani	Nigeria	Nigerian
Kenya	Kenyan	North Korea	North Korean
Kuwait	Kuwaiti	Norway	Norwegian
Kyrgyzstan	Kyrgyzstani		
		Oman	Omani
Laos	Laotian		
Latvia	Latvian	Pakistan	Pakistani
Lebanon	Lebanese	Panama	Panamanian
Lesotho	Basotho	Papua New Guinea	Papua New Guinean or Papuan
Liberia	Liberian		
Libya	Libyan		
Liechtenstein	Liechtensteiner	Paraguay	Paraguayan
Lithuania	Lithuanian	Peru	Peruvian

Some countries and their people   114

Country	Person	Country	Person
Philippines	Filipino (male) or Filipina (female)	Switzerland	Swiss
		Syria	Syrian
Poland	Pole		
Portugal	Portuguese	Taiwan	Taiwanese
Puerto Rico	Puerto Rican	Tajikistan	Tajik or Tajikistani
		Tanzania	Tanzanian
Qatar	Qatari	Thailand	Thai or Thailander
		Tonga	Tongan
Romania	Romanian	Trinidad and	Trinidadian;
Russia	Russian	Tobago	Tobagonian
Rwanda	Rwandan	Tunisia	Tunisian
		Turkey	Turk
Samoa	Samoan	Turkmenistan	Turkoman or Turkman
Saudi Arabia	Saudi or Saudi Arabian		
Senegal	Senegalese	Uganda	Ugandan
Serbia	Serbian	Ukraine	Ukrainian
Seychelles	Seychellois	United Arab	Emirati
Sierra Leone	Sierra Leonian	Emirates	
Singapore	Singaporean	United Kingdom	Briton
Slovakia	Slovak or Slovakian	(UK)	
Slovenia	Slovene or Slovenian	United States of America (USA)	American
Somalia	Somalian	Uruguay	Uruguayan
South Africa	South African	Uzbekistan	Uzbek
South Korea	South Korean		
Spain	Spaniard	Venezuela	Venezuelan
Sri Lanka	Sri Lankan	Vietnam	Vietnamese
Sudan	Sudanese		
Suriname	Surinamer	Yemen	Yemeni
Swaziland	Swazi	Zambia	Zambian
Sweden	Swede	Zimbabwe	Zimbabwean

Continent	Person	Continent	Person
Africa	African	Europe	European
Antarctica		North America	North American
Asia	Asian	South America	South American
Australia	Australian		

Numbers

	Cardinal		Ordinal			Roman
1	one	s	first	ly, s	1st	I
2	two	s	second	ly, s	2nd	II
3	three	s	third	ly, s	3rd	III
4	four	s	fourth	ly, s	4th	IV
5	five	s	fifth	ly, s	5th	V
6	six	es	sixth	ly, s	6th	VI
7	seven	s	seventh	ly, s	7th	VII
8	eight	s	eighth	ly, s	8th	VIII
9	nine	s	ninth	ly, s	9th	IX
10	ten	s	tenth	ly, s	10th	X
11	eleven	s	eleventh	s	11th	XI
12	twelve	s	twelfth	s	12th	XII
13	thirteen	s	thirteenth	s	13th	XIII
14	fourteen	s	fourteenth	s	14th	XIV
15	fifteen	s	fifteenth	s	15th	XV
16	sixteen	s	sixteenth	s	16th	XVI
17	seventeen	s	seventeenth	s	17th	XVII
18	eighteen	s	eighteenth	s	18th	XVIII
19	nineteen	s	nineteenth	s	19th	XIX
20	twenty	ies	twentieth	s	20th	XX
21	twenty-one	s	twenty-first	s	21st	XXI
22	twenty-two	s	twenty-second	s	22nd	XXII
23	twenty-three	s	twenty-third	s	23rd	XXIII
24	twenty-four	s	twenty-fourth	s	24th	XXIV
25	twenty-five	s	twenty-fifth	s	25th	XXV
26	twenty-six	es	twenty-sixth	s	26th	XXVI
27	twenty-seven	s	twenty-seventh	s	27th	XXVII
28	twenty-eight	s	twenty-eighth	s	28th	XXVIII
29	twenty-nine	s	twenty-ninth	s	29th	XXIX
30	thirty	ies	thirtieth	s	30th	XXX
31	thirty-one	s	thirty-first	s	31st	XXXI

	Cardinal		Ordinal			Roman
40	fort*y*	*ies*	fortieth	*s*	40th	XL
41	forty-one	*s*	forty-first	*s*	41st	XLI
50	fift*y*	*ies*	fiftieth	*s*	50th	L
51	fifty-one	*s*	fifty-first	*s*	51st	LI
60	sixt*y*	*ies*	sixtieth	*s*	60th	LX
61	sixty-one	*s*	sixty-first	*s*	61st	LXI
70	sevent*y*	*ies*	seventieth	*s*	70th	LXX
71	seventy-one	*s*	seventy-first	*s*	71st	LXXI
80	eight*y*	*ies*	eightieth	*s*	80th	LXXX
81	eighty-one	*s*	eighty-first	*s*	81st	LXXXI
90	ninet*y*	*ies*	ninetieth	*s*	90th	XC
91	ninety-one	*s*	ninety-first	*s*	91st	XCI
100	hundred	*s*	hundredth	*s*	100th	C
500	five hundred		five hundreth		500th	D
1,000	thousand	*s*	thousandth	*s*	1,000th	M
10,000	ten thousand		ten thousandth		10,000th	
100,000	one hundred thousand		one hundred thousandth		100,000th	
1,000,000	million	*s*	millionth	*s*	1,000,000th	

Roman numerals

When a smaller number comes *before* a larger one, it is subtracted, eg
IV = 5 − 1 = 4; IX = 10 − 1 = 9; XL = 50 − 10 = 40; CD = 500 − 100 = 400
When a smaller number comes *after* a larger one, it is added, eg
VI = 5 + 1 = 6; XI = 10 + 1 = 11; LX = 50 + 10 = 60; DC = 500 + 100 = 600

Contractions (shortened words)

These are words which have been shortened by joining two words together and placing an apostrophe where a letter or letters have been left out. Learn the words and the contractions, being very careful to remember exactly where the apostrophe goes.

can't = cannot
don't = do not
won't = will not
isn't = is not
aren't = are not
didn't = did not
hadn't = had not
hasn't = has not
wasn't = was not
shan't = shall not
doesn't = does not
haven't = have not
mustn't = must not
needn't = need not
weren't = were not
couldn't = could not
wouldn't = would not
shouldn't = should not

he's = he is; he has
she's = she is; she has
it's = it is
who's = who is
that's = that is
what's = what is
here's = here is
there's = there is

I'll = I will; I shall
we'll = we will; we shall
he'll = he will; he shall
she'll = she will; she shall
you'll = you will; you shall
who'll = who will; who shall
they'll = they will; they shall

I'd = I had; I would
he'd = he had; he would
we'd = we had; we would
you'd = you had; you would
who'd = who had; who would
they'd = they had; they would

we're = we are
you're = you are
who're = who are
they're = they are

I've = I have
we've = we have
you've = you have
they've = they have

I'm = I am

The apostrophe is also used to show possession, eg

| The boy's book; | girl's coat; | man's car; | woman's watch. |
| The boys' books; | girls' coats; | men's cars; | women's watches. |

Homophones

These are words that sound alike but have different meanings and spellings.

accept	(receive)	cereal	(wheat, oats, etc)	foul	(dirty; unfair)
except	(leaving out)	serial	(in parts, as story,	fowl	(bird)
aisle	(space between		film, etc)	freeze	(turn into ice)
	rows)	cheap	(not dear)	frieze	(wall decoration)
I'll	(I will; I shall)	cheep	(bird sound)	groan	(moan)
isle	(island)	chute	(a slide)	grown	(got bigger)
allowed	(let; permitted)	shoot	(fire)	guessed	(guess)
aloud	(not quietly)	core	(middle of apple,	guest	(visitor)
altar	(religious table)		etc)	hair	(of head)
alter	(change)	corps	(group of cadets,	hare	(animal)
arc	(curve)		etc)	hall	(room; passage)
ark	(boat)	crevasse	(crack in glacier)	haul	(pull; amount
bare	(naked; empty)	crevice	(crack in rock or		taken)
bear	(animal; carry;		wall)	hart	(stag)
	endure)	cue	(hint; snooker	heart	(of body)
baron	(lord)		stick)	heal	(cure)
barren	(bare; empty)	queue	(line of persons,	heel	(of foot)
beach	(seashore)		etc)	hear	(listen)
beech	(tree)	currant	(fruit)	here	(in this place)
bean	(plant)	current	(flow of water, etc)	heard	(listened)
been	(past of be)	cygnet	(young swan)	herd	(of cattle, etc)
blew	(blow)	signet	(a seal, ring)	higher	(taller)
blue	(colour)	dear	(beloved; costly)	hire	(rent)
board	(wood; go on ship;	deer	(animal)	him	(he)
	lodge)	desert	(sandy place; run	hymn	(song of praise)
bored	(weary; drilled		away)	hoard	(hidden store)
	hole)	dessert	(pudding)	horde	(crowd)
bough	(branch)	die	(lose life)	hoarse	(husky)
bow	(bend)	dye	(colour)	horse	(animal)
brake	(to stop)	draft	(a rough plan)	hole	(hollow place)
break	(to snap)	draught	(flow of cold air)	whole	(all; complete)
buy	(purchase)	fair	(just; light;	hour	(sixty minutes)
by	(near to, etc)		entertainment)	our	(belonging to us)
bye	(run in cricket;	fare	(price of journey;	it's	(it is; it has)
	goodbye)		food)	its	(belonging to it)
ceiling	(roof of room)	farther	(further)	knew	(know)
sealing	(fastening)	father	(male parent)	new	(just made)
cent	(coin)	flour	(ground wheat)	knight	(Sir)
scent	(smell; perfume)	flower	(blossom)	night	(opposite of day)
sent	(send)	fort	(castle)		
		fought	(fight)		

knot	(tied string; sea speed)	place	(position; put)	tire	(weary)
		plaice	(fish)	tyre	(wheel cover)
not	(no)	pray	(ask a god)	to	(towards)
know	(understand)	prey	(victim; thing hunted)	too	(also; more than enough)
no	(not any; opposite of yes)	program	(for a computer)	two	(number)
lain	(lie flat)	programme	(on television; for concert)	wait	(stay; serve)
lane	(narrow path)			weight	(heaviness)
leant	(leaned)	rain	(water)	waste	(not used; useless)
lent	(lend)	reign	(rule)		
made	(make)	rein	(strap)	waist	(of body)
maid	(girl)	rap	(knock)	way	(direction; manner; road)
mare	(female horse)	wrap	(cover)		
mayor	(head of town)	ring	(circle; bell sound)	weigh	(measure heaviness)
meat	(flesh)	wring	(twist)		
meet	(come together)	road	(highway)	weak	(not strong)
medal	(badge – for bravery, etc)	rode	(ride)	week	(seven days)
		rowed	(used oars)	weather	(climate)
meddle	(interfere)	sail	(travel by ship)	whether	(if)
meter	(measuring device)	sale	(selling)	which	(what one?; who?)
metre	(length measure)	scene	(view; place)	witch	(woman using magic)
moan	(groan)	seen	(noticed)		
mown	(cut grass, etc)	shore	(seashore)	who's	(who is; who has)
muscle	(of body)	sure	(certain)	whose	(belonging to whom)
mussel	(shellfish)	slay	(kill)		
one	(single)	sleigh	(sledge)	wood	(timber)
won	(win)	stair	(step)	would	(past of will)
pail	(bucket)	stare	(look at)	you're	(you are)
pale	(faint; whitish)	steal	(thieve)	your	(belonging to you)
pain	(suffering)	steel	(metal)		
pane	(sheet of glass)	tail	(end)		
pair	(two)	tale	(story)		
pare	(cut away; peel)	their	(belonging to them)		
pear	(fruit)	there	(in that place)		
passed	(pass)	they're	(they are)		
past	(time gone by)	theirs	(belonging to them)		
peace	(quiet)	there's	(there is)		
piece	(a part)	threw	(throw)		
pedal	(foot lever)	through	(from end to end)		
peddle	(to sell things at door)	throne	(king's or queen's seat)		
peer	(stare)	thrown	(throw)		
pier	(jetty)				

Spelling lists of words to learn

The following lists contain the words you will need to use most often in your writing and compositions. You should, therefore, learn and try to remember how to spell all these words. Choose the shortest and easiest words at the beginning of each section to learn first. It is better to learn a few words each day rather than a long list, at one time, once a week. To make it easier for you the words are usually arranged in lists according to the number of letters in the words: three, four, five letters, etc. The number at the top of a word list shows the number of letters in each word in that list. Before you start to learn a list of words, first study all the words in the list and notice that some words have the same letters in exactly the same order as others in the list.

All the words on pages 121 to 126 and at the bottom of page 129 are verbs, or may be used as verbs, and are arranged in lists according to the way in which their *ed, ing, s* endings are formed. When your teacher tests you on the words you have learnt he or she will probably ask you how to spell some of these words with their *ed, ing, s* endings to see whether you have understood this, eg

bark	**scare**	**drop**
mark*ed*	**score***d*	**chop***ped*
park*ing*	**stor***ing*	**shop***ping*
work*s*	**stone***s*	**stop***s*

First make sure that you know how to spell all the words at the bottom of this page as you will need to use these words in your written work much more often than any other words.

3	3	3	4	4	4	4	5
all	did	our	back	home	only	want	after
and	had	out	been	into	over	went	about
are	has	saw	call	just	play	were	house
big	her	see	came	like	said	what	could
boy	him	she	come	look	some	when	would
but	his	the	down	made	than	well	where
can	how	was	from	make	that	will	which
for	now	who	girl	more	them	with	other
get	not	why	have	much	then	work	their*
got	off	you	here	must	this	your	there*

* their (belonging to them – their toys)
* there (in that place – it is over there)
* they're (they are – they are playing)

You may add *ed*, *ing*, *s* to all the following words, eg

        cook   *ed*, *ing*, *s* = **cooked, cooking, cooks**

3		4		4		4	
act	*ed, ing, s*	book	*ed, ing, s*	back	*ed, ing, s*	camp	*ed, ing, s*
add		cook		pack		damp	
air		hook		sack		bump	
arm		look		dock		dump	
ask		cool		lock		jump	
end		pool		rock		lump	
ink		show		kick		pump	
oil		slow		lick		bomb	
own		flow		pick		comb	
toy		snow		tick		lamb	

4		4		4		4	
dust	*ed, ing, s*	call	*ed, ing, s*	bark	*ed, ing, s*	load	*ed, ing, s*
last		fell		mark		boat	
list		well		park		coat	
nest		yell		work		roar	
rest		fill		cork		soap	
test		kill		fork		help	
post		mill		milk		long	
lift		will		talk		hunt	
melt		pull		walk		want	
salt		roll		bank		word	

4		4		4		4	
form	*ed, ing, s*	gain	*ed, ing, s*	head	*ed, ing, s*	bath	*ed, ing, s*
farm		pain		heal		down	
harm		rain		heat		even	
warm		pair		seat		open	
band		fail		fear		turn	
hand		jail		near		join	
land		nail		team		iron	
sand		sail		play		part	
bang		tail		pray		mind	
gang		wait		stay		view	

5		5		5		6	
clean	*ed, ing, s*	knock	*ed, ing, s*	thank	*ed, ing, s*	answer	*ed, ing, s*
clear		clock		train		corner	
climb		block		tramp		flower	
cloud		shock		treat		bother	
clown		black		light		gather	
chain		crack		right		matter	
chair		track		sight		master	
chalk		brick		dream		murder	
cheer		trick		radio		number	
cheat		wreck		visit		wonder	

5		5		6		6	
enter	*ed, ing, s*	count	*ed, ing, s*	appear	*ed, ing, s*	record	*ed, ing, s*
cover		cough		arrest		return	
lower		rough		attack		reward	
offer		round		happen		school	
order		pound		hollow		scream	
water		sound		follow		stream	
paper		mouth		borrow		belong	
paint		group		button		poison	
point		scout		butter		powder	
plant		shout		letter		obtain	

5		5		6		7	
laugh	*ed, ing, s*	boast	*ed, ing, s*	colour	*ed, ing, s*	explain	*ed, ing, s*
haunt		coast		doctor		contain	
field		roast		ground		curtain	
float		toast		garden		captain	
floor		start		awaken		holiday	
flood		stamp		fasten		journey	
bloom		storm		listen		present	
stoop		allow		pocket		pretend	
spoon		enjoy		rocket		soldier	
sport		guard		ticket		station	

5		6+		6+		7+	
crawl	*ed, ing, s*	expect	*ed, ing, s*	repair	*ed, ing, s*	disobey	*ed, ing, s*
creak		collect		remain		discover	
crowd		correct		remind		disappear	
crown		protect		remember		disappoint	

You may add *ing* and *s* to the following words. You may not add *ed*. The words on the right of the columns are used instead.

buy	*ing, s*	: bought	wear	*ing, s*	: wore, worn
lay		: laid	ring		: rang, rung
pay		: paid	sing		: sang, sung
say		: said	spring		: sprang, sprung
cost		: cost	sink		: sank, sunk
feed		: fed	drink		: drank, drunk
feel		: felt	think		: thought
find		: found	bring		: brought
hear		: heard	fight		: fought
hold		: held	build		: built
hurt	*ing, s*	: hurt	shoot	*ing, s*	: shot
keep		: kept	sleep		: slept
lead		: led	stand		: stood
lend		: lent	spend		: spent
send		: sent	sweep		: swept
sell		: sold	swing		: swung
tell		: told	spread		: spread
meet		: met	break		: broke, broken
mean		: meant	speak		: spoke, spoken
read		: read	steal		: stole, stolen
see	*n, ing, s*	: saw	eat	*en, ing, s*	: ate
blow	*n, ing, s*	: blew	beat	*en, ing, s*	: beat
draw	*n, ing, s*	: drew	fall	*en, ing, s*	: fell
grow	*n, ing, s*	: grew			
know	*n, ing, s*	: knew	catch	*ing, es*	: caught
throw	*n, ing, s*	: threw	teach	*ing, es*	: taught

You may add *ed*, *ing*, *es* to all the following words:

box *ed, ing, es*	fish *ed, ing, es*	kiss *ed, ing, es*	hatch *ed, ing, es*
fix	dish	miss	latch
mix	push	cross	match
	rush	pass	patch
	wash	class	watch
	wish	grass	scratch
	brush	guess	fetch
	crash	press	hitch
	flash	dress	pitch
	finish	address	stitch

bunch *ed, ing, es*
hunch
lunch
munch
punch
crunch
march
reach
search
touch

All the following words end in a consonant followed by a letter **e**.
You may add *d* and *s* to all the words but the **e** must be dropped before adding *ing*, eg

hope   *d*, *ɇing*, *s* = **hoped, hoping, hopes**

4	4	4	5
care *d, ɇing, s*	dive *d, ɇing, s*	hope *d, ɇing, s*	argue *d, ɇing, s*
dare	tire	rope	blame
face	fire	note	flame
race	wire	hole	place
save	wipe	love	dance
wave	fine	move	piece
hate	line	name	force
bake	live	side	voice
rake	like	time	price
wake	hike	type	prize

5		5		6		6	
chase	d, ɇing, s	scare	d, ɇing, s	battle	d, ɇing, s	arrive	d, ɇing, s
close		score		bottle		behave	
cause		store		settle		chance	
pause		stone		bubble		bridge	
house		smile		paddle		change	
amuse		serve		puzzle		charge	
raise		taste		bundle		garage	
nurse		waste		double		damage	
sense		brave		hurdle		manage	
tease		prove		single		voyage	

6		7		7		8	
decide	d, ɇing, s	balance	d, ɇing, s	picture	d, ɇing, s	surprise	d, ɇing, s
divide		bandage		promise		exercise	
invite		believe		provide		exchange	
escape		bicycle		prepare		celebrate	
notice		breathe		produce		continue	
excuse		deserve		grumble		decorate	
refuse		capture		stumble		describe	
rescue		explore		tremble		puncture	
circle		imagine		trouble		struggle	
centre		receive		whistle		treasure	

All the words in the left-hand columns end in a consonant followed by a letter **e**. You may add *s* to all the words but the **e** must be dropped before adding *ing*.
You may not add *d*. The words on the right of the column are used instead.

come	ɇing, s	: came	bite	ɇing, s	: bit, bitten
make		: made	hide		: hid, hidden
lose		: lost	ride		: rode, ridden
leave		: left	rise		: rose, risen
slide		: slid	drive		: drove, driven
strike		: struck	write		: wrote, written
			choose		: chose, chosen

give	n, ɇing, s	: gave
take	n, ɇing, s	: took
shake	n, ɇing, s	: shook
mistake	n, ɇing, s	: mistook

You may add *s* to all the following words. The final consonant (the last letter) must be doubled before adding *ed*, *ing*, eg

drop   *ped*, *ping*, s = **dropped, dropping, drops**

3		3		3		4	
bat	*ted, ting, s*	**dip**	*ped, ping, s*	**beg**	*ged, ging, s*	**drop**	*ped, ping, s*
pat		**rip**		**peg**		**chop**	
pet		**tip**		**gag**		**shop**	
net		**zip**		**wag**		**stop**	
wet		**hop**		**hug**		**swop**	
fit		**pop**		**tug**		**ship**	
rot		**top**		**gun**	*ned, ning, s*	**slip**	
rob	*bed, bing, s*	**tap**		**sun**		**skip**	
mob		**map**		**pin**		**drip**	
sob		**yap**		**jab**	*bed, bing, s*	**grip**	

4		4		5+		5+	
trip	*ped, ping, s*	**plan**	*ned, ning, s*	**equal**	*led, ling, s*	**admit**	*ted, ting, s*
whip		**stun**		**signal**		**permit**	
clap		**grin**		**pencil**		**commit**	
snap		**skin**		**model**		**regret**	
trap		**skid**	*ded, ding, s*	**cancel**		**occur**	*red, ring, s*
wrap		**chat**	*ted, ting, s*	**parcel**		**refer**	
step		**plot**		**shovel**		**prefer**	
stab	*bed, bing, s*	**knot**		**travel**		**equip**	*ped, ping, s*
grab		**knit**		**tunnel**		**kidnap**	
drag	*ged, ging, s*	**dial**	*led, ling, s*	**quarrel**		**unwrap**	

None of the following words may end in *ed*.
The words in the right hand column are used instead.

get	*ting, s* : **got**		**dig**	*ging, s* : **dug**	
set	*ting, s* : **set**		**run**	*ning, s* : **ran**	
sit	*ting, s* : **sat**		**win**	*ning, s* : **won**	
hit	*ting, s* : **hit**		**spin**	*ning, s* : **spun**	
cut	*ting, s* : **cut**		**begin**	*ning, s* : **began, begun**	
shut	*ting, s* : **shut**		**swim**	*ming, s* : **swam, swum**	

You may add *er, est, ly, ness* to all the following words, eg

    bold   *er, est, ly, ness* = **bolder, boldest, boldly, boldness**

4		4+		5	
bold	*er, est, ly, ness*	**fair**	*er, est, ly, ness*	**light**	*er, est, ly, ness*
cold		**dear**		**tight**	
poor		**near**		**quick**	
cool		**neat**		**quiet**	
deep		**mean**		**queer**	
dark		**weak**		**steep**	
kind		**clean**		**sharp**	
loud		**clear**		**short**	
rich		**cheap**		**smart**	
slow		**great**		**thick**	
soft		**fresh**		**rough**	
wild		**clever**		**tough**	

You may add *r, st, ly, ness* to the following words:

4		4+	
late	*r, st, ly, ness*	**rude**	*r, st, ly, ness*
nice		**wide**	
fine		**large**	
safe		**close**	
sore		**fierce**	
sure		**strange**	

You may add *ly, ness* to the following words but the last letter must be doubled before adding *er, est*.

3		3+	
sad	*der, dest, ly, ness*	**fat**	*ter, test, ly, ness*
mad	*der, dest, ly, ness*	**flat**	*ter, test, ly, ness*
hot	*ter, test, ly, ness*	**thin**	*ner, nest, ly, ness*
fit	*ter, test, ly, ness*		

All the following words end in *y*.
The *y* must be dropped before adding *ier, iest, ily, iness,* eg

happ*y*   *ier, iest, ily, iness* = **happier, happiest, happily, happiness**

4+		5	
eas*y*	*ier, iest, ily, iness*	happ*y*	*ier, iest, ily, iness*
laz*y*		sunn*y*	
tid*y*		funn*y*	
tin*y*		fuss*y*	
ugl*y*		mess*y*	
dirt*y*		mudd*y*	
empt*y*		joll*y*	
heav*y*		sill*y*	
juic*y*		sorr*y*	
luck*y*		shak*y*	
nois*y*		wear*y*	
rock*y*		wind*y*	

6		6+	
stick*y*	*ier, iest, ily, iness*	clums*y*	*ier, iest, ily, iness*
trick*y*		cloud*y*	
shabb*y*		chill*y*	
prett*y*		hungr*y*	
bounc*y*		kindl*y*	
costl*y*		stead*y*	
sleep*y*		untid*y*	
greed*y*		unluck*y*	
cheek*y*		naught*y*	
breez*y*		thirst*y*	
gloom*y*		health*y*	
storm*y*		wealth*y*	

4+	
bus*y*	*ier, iest, ily*
angr*y*	*ier, iest, ily*
earl*y*	*ier, iest, iness*
lonel*y*	*ier, iest, iness*
sand*y*	*ier, iest, iness*
merr*y*	*ier, iest, ily, iment*
lovel*y*	*ier, iest, iness*

				Days
dough	also	Monday	January	31
cough	always	Tuesday	February	28/29
rough	almost	Wednesday	March	31
tough	although	Thursday	April	30
enough	already	Friday	May	31
plough	altogether	Saturday	June	30
through		Sunday	July	31
ought	all right		August	31
bought		spring	September	30
brought		summer	October	31
fought		autumn	November	30
thought		winter	December	31

All the following words end in **y**.
You may add *ing* but the **y** must be dropped before adding *ied*, *ies*.

cry	ing	carry	ing	copy	ing
cr*ied*	ies	carr*ied*	ies	cop*ied*	ies
dry	ing	marry	ing	bury	ing
dr*ied*	ies	marr*ied*	ies	bur*ied*	ies
try	ing	hurry	ing	tidy	ing
tr*ied*	ies	hurr*ied*	ies	tid*ied*	ies
fry	ing	worry	ing	occupy	ing
fr*ied*	ies	worr*ied*	ies	occup*ied*	ies
spy	ing	empty	ing	satisfy	ing
sp*ied*	ies	empt*ied*	ies	satisf*ied*	ies
fly	ing	study	ing	terrify	ing
fl*ies*		stud*ied*	ies	terrif*ied*	ies
flew, flown					

A very few verbs end in *ie*. You may add *d* and *s* but the **ie** must be changed to **y** before adding *ing*.

die	d, s	lie	d, s	tie	d, s
dy*ing*		ly*ing*		ty*ing*	

All the words in the left-hand columns are singular nouns. The words in the right-hand columns are plurals, which you use when there is more than one.

Singular		Plural	Singular	Plural	Singular	Plural
foot		feet	bab*y*	ies	key	s
goose		geese	lad*y*	ies	donkey	s
tooth		teeth	bod*y*	ies	monkey	s
mouse		mice	pon*y*	ies	valley	s
man		men	cit*y*	ies	chimney	s
woman		women	arm*y*	ies	cowboy	s
child		children	nav*y*	ies	railway	s
			aunt*y*	ies	gangway	s
life		lives	dadd*y*	ies	holiday	s
wife		wives	mumm*y*	ies	birthday	s
knife		knives				
			dais*y*	ies	zoo	s
leaf		leaves	dair*y*	ies	piano	s
loaf		loaves	fair*y*	ies	radio	s
thief		thieves	stor*y*	ies		
			part*y*	ies	echo	es
dwarf	*s* or	dwarves	jell*y*	ies	hero	es
scarf	*s* or	scarves	lorr*y*	ies	cargo	es
wharf	*s* or	wharves	pupp*y*	ies	potato	es
hoof	*s* or	hooves	hobb*y*	ies	tomato	es
roof	*s*		enem*y*	ies	volcano	es
elf		elves	canar*y*	ies	bus	es
calf		calves	famil*y*	ies	glass	es
half		halves	grann*y*	ies	beach	es
wolf		wolves	cherr*y*	ies	peach	es
shelf		shelves	countr*y*	ies	torch	es
			librar*y*	ies	witch	es
self		selves	factor*y*	ies	church	es
itself			robber*y*	ies	circus	es
myself			myster*y*	ies	princess	es
himself			discover*y*	ies	sandwich	es
herself						
yourself		yourselves	every	*body, one, thing, where*		
		ourselves	any	*body, one, thing, where, how, way*		
		themselves	some	*body, one, thing, where, how, times*		

4	4	5	4		4		5	
able	than	these	bell	s	bird	s	giant	s
away	that	those	ball	s	desk	s	glove	s
best	then	where	wall	s	lake	s	green	s
born	them	which	hall	s	lawn	s	hedge	s
both	they	while	hill	s	lion	s	horse	s
does	this	whole	cake	s	neck	s	hotel	s
done	true	whose	card	s	nose	s	jewel	s
goes	luck	worse	cart	s	page	s	lemon	s
gone	ever	worst	cave	s	path	s	noise	s
gold	very	worth	case	s	pond	s	ocean	s

4	4	5	4		4		5	
dead	went	could	coal	s	shed	s	other	s
deaf	were	would	goal	s	shoe	s	owner	s
each	what	magic	door	s	sock	s	plate	s
else	when	might	food	s	song	s	fruit	s
just	with	money	moon	s	tent	s	pupil	s
must	clay	music	room	s	town	s	purse	s
much	beef	never	wood	s	tree	s	queen	s
many	pork	pence	wool	s	mile	s	salad	s
more	east	sugar	flag	s	your	s	shirt	s
most	west	ready	frog	s	year	s	snake	s

4	5	5	4		5		5	
from	about	among	game	s	apple	s	stair	s
next	above	below	gate	s	baker	s	stick	s
none	after	blood	gift	s	bread	s	stove	s
only	again	earth	hole	s	beast	s	sword	s
once	ahead	often	home	s	cabin	s	table	s
upon	alone	sorry	hour	s	cloth	s	thing	s
same	along	sheep	king	s	comic	s	tiger	s
some	alike	shall	kite	s	dozen	s	truck	s
soon	alive	under	knee	s	front	s	white	s
such	aside	until	idea	s	ghost	s	world	s

6	7	6		6		9	
across	against	friend	s	infant	s	adventure	s
afraid	another	forest	s	insect	s	aeroplane	s
around	because	finger	s	inside	s	afternoon	s
asleep	beneath	father	s	island	s	chocolate	s
ashore	between	mother	s	desert	s	favourite	s
awhile	clothes	leader	s	orange	s	passenger	s
before	instead	reader	s	second	s	newspaper	s
behind	nothing	saucer	s	minute	s	orchestra	s
better	perhaps	sister	s	moment	s	programme	s
cattle	without	reason	s	museum	s	vegetable	s

6	8	6		7		full	y
during	together	bullet	s	bedroom	s	awful	ly
either	tomorrow	carrot	s	blanket	s	useful	ly
famous	horrible	coffee	s	brother	s	careful	ly
hardly	horribly	cotton	s	teacher	s	playful	ly
little	terrible	dinner	s	sausage	s	cheerful	ly
middle	terribly	kitten	s	cabbage	s	dreadful	ly
modern	possible	lesson	s	cottage	s	thankful	ly
unless	possibly	rabbit	s	message	s	beautiful	ly
utmost	probable	robber	s	village	s	forgetful	ly
within	probably	rubber	s	lettuce	s	wonderful	ly

6	6		6		7			
people	animal	s	parent	s	chicken	s	helpful	ly
petrol	banana	s	person	s	kitchen	s	hopeful	ly
plenty	beside	s	prince	s	husband	s	skilful	ly
police	bucket	s	secret	s	pudding	s	faithful	ly
rather	castle	s	street	s	morning	s	grateful	ly
really	cousin	s	string	s	evening	s	peaceful	ly
safety	coward	s	violin	s	tadpole	s	powerful	ly
should	danger	s	window	s	tractor	s	spiteful	ly
seldom	engine	s	pillow	s	visitor	s	delightful	ly
silver	needle	s	yellow	s	outside	s	disgraceful	ly

133

Index

Index